# JOURNEY TO
# DAY BEFORE YESTERDAY

# E. R. EASTMAN

# JOURNEY TO
# DAY BEFORE YESTERDAY

## drawings by Paul Frame

PRENTICE-HALL, INC., Englewood Cliffs, N.J.

Prentice-Hall International, Inc. (*London, Tokyo, Sydney, Paris*). Prentice-Hall of Canada, Ltd. Prentice-Hall de Mexico, S. A.

OTHER BOOKS BY E. R. EASTMAN

*The Trouble Maker*

*These Changing Times*

*Growing Up in the Horse and Buggy Days* (written
  with Carl E. Ladd)

*Tough Sod*

*The Destroyers*

*The Settlers*

*No Drums*

*Not with Dreams*

*Walking the Broad Highway*

*Hostages to Fortune*

*The Words and the Music*

*How to Speak and Write for Rural Audiences*

*Eastman's Chestnuts Vols. I-V*

To my wife—Belle Rockefeller Eastman.

WITH GRATITUDE AND APPRECIATION I ACKNOWLEDGE all of the help I have had in preparing the manuscript and assembling the illustrations for this book. Without this help, the personal and intimate stories right out of the actual experiences and lives of so many of my relatives, neighbors and friends could not have been written.

In particular, I want to acknowledge the lifelong contribution of my wife, Belle Rockefeller Eastman, with whom I have shared so many experiences both of Day Before Yesterday and of Today; to Donald, George, and Robert, our sons, and their wives, Lucile, Eleanor and Tenney—all of whom have given me constant support and understanding in all of my writings.

To Margaret Roe, our cousin, who helped so much in the research for this book and who took all my first dictation in her rapid longhand. Margaret's unusual memory of people and events of the horse and buggy days has been of untold assistance.

To Mrs. Esther Wilcox, my secretary, who has been of invaluable help with constructive suggestions and in the typing and editing of the manuscript; and to Mrs. Sue Hastings and Mrs. Eileen Kohles who typed and re-typed many chapters.

I am deeply indebted also to Dr. Earl E. Clarke, Dean of Students at Ithaca College who read most of the manuscript for this book and who visited with me for hours about his own experiences as a boy growing up on a ranch in North Dakota.

To Frederick L. Rath, Vice Director of the New York Historical Association, with whom we spent a most delightful and profitable day at the famous Fenimore House and Farmers' Museum at Cooperstown, and who loaned me many of the most interesting illustrations for the book.

To Herschel D. Newsom, Master of the National

Grange, who filled me in on some of the history and background of the Grange.

To Prof. Elmer S. Phillips who took time to go over hundreds of the pictures at the New York State College of Agriculture and loaned me those that I chose for this book.

To William Heidt of the DeWitt Historical Association at Ithaca, N. Y. who went all out to help Margaret Roe and me get suitable illustrations.

To Paul Taber of the G.L.F. who read and corrected some of the manuscript.

To Roland W. Olson in the Public Relations Department of the Farmers Union who gave me detailed information about his great organization.

To Gordon Conklin, editor of American Agriculturist, who loaned me many pictures for the book.

To Cornell University Press for permission to quote from Dean Isaac Roberts' *Autobiography of a Farm Boy*.

To Prof. William B. Ward, Head of the Extension Teaching and Information Service at Cornell University, who furnished an almost unlimited amount of background material.

To Joseph Hanrahan of the Ithaca Engraving Company who advised me on the procedure for the reproduction of pictures.

To C. Hadley Smith who did an outstanding and expert job in re-photographing old pictures so that they could be reproduced.

To my friend Clinton R. Wilcox who traveled with me, took some of the pictures, and whose interest in the project was always an inspiration.

To the more than 200 readers of American Agriculturist who sent me pictures of Day Before Yesterday people and scenes for possible reproduction in the book.

To Mr. William J. Waters, editor of *The Ithaca Journal* who gave me permission to quote at length from my weekly column, "Let's Visit Awhile," in *The Ithaca Journal*.

To my friend, Dr. Carroll V. Newsom, a longtime associate in education who encouraged me to put in writing these memories and experiences of other days.

Finally, I acknowledge my debt to all those friends of Day Before Yesterday whom I knew and loved and with whom I walked the Great Highway.

And to my family and friends of Today who are a constant source of encouragement and inspiration.

# CONTENTS

# JOURNEY TO
# DAY BEFORE YESTERDAY

# CHAPTER ONE

# "BORNING GROUND"

O NE SUMMER DAY RECENTLY, I TURNED OFF THE main highway, drove up a hill and turned onto a private farm road. After a mile or so, I came to an abandoned farm to what the Vermonters very appropriately call my "borning ground." So high is the place, that it seemed to me I could almost reach up and touch the fleecy clouds. As I stood there on that summer day in the quiet—so hard to attain in these noisy, modern times—I was flooded with memories. I took my hat off, for it seemed to me that I had never been closer to God.

Remembered were Mother's stories of how she and Father, a young married couple with two little boys, had come to that lonesome hill farm and how hard they had had to work for the bare necessities of life for themselves, their two boys, and later my younger brother and myself who were born there.

Probably because I love to get into a big blackberry slashing when the berries, big as the end of your thumb, hang heavily on the high bushes, I have always remembered Father's story of going blackberrying when he had first come to that farm. After a day's work in the fields, when the chores were done, he would take a 14-quart milk pail after supper and go a short distance to a slashing where the berries were so large and thick that he could fill his pail before dark.

I know how pleased Mother was to get those berries. Together with thousands of other farm women, she took great pride in the long rows of canned fruits and vegetables, processed during the summer in the hot farm kitchen, to supplement the meager diet of the long winter months. The cellar was the first place Mother took a visiting woman, to point with pride to the results of her hard summer's work. Who shall say that her achievement—and similar ones by other women—was not as great as any of those in modern days when we live by can-openers and refrigerators?

Long gone was the house where a home had been. The place was overgrown with brush and weeds, but there was still a lilac bush which I am sure Mother had planted, testifying to the love of beauty which springs eternal in a woman's heart.

Yes, every material thing of value is gone from the old homestead except the lilac bush, but the spirit of that home and the memories of Father, Mother, and brothers who lived, worked, adventured and loved there will always be green.

Across the abandoned road where the big barn had stood, a spring was still pouring water into a broken trough. I drank of its waters. It couldn't restore my youth, but it was good to remember that those whom I had loved long since had refreshed themselves at that same spring. Marking the boundaries of the barnyard was a stone wall, the stones of which had undoubtedly been laid by my father's hands. What tremendous hand-labors our ancestors performed in building the stone walls and rail fences across America!

How well I remember that stone wall. On one of the rare occasions when Mother had a hired girl, the two were helping Father and my older brothers with

Within the memory of men still living, oxen were in use. My father had a yoke when I was very young. Note rail or stake fence.

the evening milking. The milk had to be carried across the barnyard over the stone wall by steps called a stile to the cool farm cellar. One night I followed Elva, the hired girl, out of the stable when she had a pailful of milk in each hand. When she started up the steps of the stile, I was right behind her, so I grabbed her ankle, and over that stone wall she plunged—milk and all—into a mess of spilled milk and mad woman. More angry than hurt, Elva set up a yell that could be heard for miles and took after me. Hearing the rumpus, Mother came running, caught me,

gave me a sound spanking, and sent me bawling to bed without supper.

I wonder how many of you who read this can remember how butter was made on farms in the days before most milk was shipped in liquid form to the cities? The big farm cellar was lined with long racks on which the milk was strained into small tin pans after it was brought from the barn. When the cream had risen, Mother skimmed it off with a small, perforated hand-skimmer and set it aside until she had enough to make a churning. The skimmed milk

3

was fed to the hogs and to the young calves.

What good cottage—or, as we used to call it, *Dutch*—cheese that skimmed milk made. I liked it so well as a very little boy that one day, when I was playing around in the hoghouse in which there was a big barrel for storing the skimmed milk for the pigs, I climbed on a potato crate and helped myself to the sour curds that had risen on the milk. But Mother caught me and gave me another spanking for eating the dirty fly-specked stuff.

Did you ever operate an old dash butter churn? Like thousands of other farm boys, I did and I hated it. I was pleased when Father got a big dog tread. Poor old Ponto, the heavy farm dog, was put on that to walk endless miles, turning the wheel which operated the churn. When the butter "came," Mother skimmed it out of the churn into a big butter bowl and worked it back and forth with a hand-ladle until all the buttermilk was out of it. Then, after adding salt, she packed it into big firkins or butter tubs, all ready to go to the market.

I pause to remark that once you had tasted that good natural farm buttermilk, nothing like it that you can buy nowadays can compare with it. Day Before Yesterday buttermilk was a favorite and whole-

This house at Deerfield, N.H. was built by Ephraim Eastman, my great-great-great-grandfather, in 1760. His great-great-grandfather Roger Eastman landed in the Massachusetts Bay Colony in 1638.

4

some farm drink. Some said that it contained a little alcohol, but although I tried, I never could get hilarious from it.

When about a week's supply of butter was packed and ready for market, Father loaded it into the democrat wagon. Then, taking my younger brother and myself with her, Mother went down the long hill to the village railroad station, where the station agent was also a representative of a butter-buying concern. Taking the tubs or firkins out of the wagon, the station agent lined them up, then plunged a long, smooth rod down through the center of the tub. When he pulled it out, it was coated with samples of each of the butter layers that Mother had packed day by day into the tub. I will always remember how that station agent licked each sample down across the rod to test the quality of each layer of butter. After wiping off the rod with a soiled rag, he repeated the process with the butter in the next tub. Bacteria or sanitary restrictions? People had heard little about them—and cared less.

And speaking of the butter bowl—last summer, my wife Belle and I were visiting a small town in the North Country of New York State. In a little antique

Skimming the cream—one of the many tasks that fell to the farm woman.

shop, there was a lovely polished wood butter bowl, which the sales clerk said would make a charming magazine holder. I ran my hand over the smooth surface, polished to such a gloss that the wood showed the beautiful red-brown mahogany, while memories of Mother's homemade butter came floating back.

My folks used to have a lot to say about the time I ran away from home when I was four or five years old on that farm where I was born. It was a base slander. I didn't run away at all. I was just trying to be of help. The truth of the matter is that I had been with my father and brothers to the far end of the farm when they were after a load of hay. Now some way or other, wild berries of any kind always intrigued me. Coming home on top of that load of hay, I noted some fine red raspberries along the fence; so as soon as I got home, I took a little pail, and, without anyone seeing me, I went back after those berries. It was a long way for a little boy with short legs and it was a hot day. So I was gone a long, long time and the whole family went out searching for me. At long last, and as it was getting dark, I came trudging up the road with maybe a dozen or so berries in the bottom of the pail. I was hungry and

had eaten most of them. Now that's the truth about my running away and I'm glad to set the record straight.

But I was not the only one of Mother's sons who caused her worry. One time when she was very busy, she asked my older brother Charlie, then in his teens, to hold Albert, my youngest brother, then a baby, on his lap. Albert apparently didn't feel well and was crying. Charlie didn't think much of the deal. There were more important things to do than help bring up a baby. So he conceived the idea that if he bounced the baby high and hard enough on his knee, the baby wouldn't have any breath left with which to cry. Unfortunately, however, Charlie sat close to an open window, and in one of the big bounces, he lost control of Albert, who plunged out the window, which, fortunately, was only a short distance from the ground. Albert got a cut on his chin, the scar of which he always carried. Charlie got a licking! You will gather from these stories that Mother believed firmly in the saying: "Spare the rod and spoil the child." Incidentally, I believe it too.

To this day, the nicest time of the day to me is twilight. Perhaps that feeling stems from the fact that

How those silo and threshing gangs could eat and eat and eat Day Before Yesterday! Mother always had enough, although a small boy often wondered if there would be anything left for him.

Mother used to pause from the day's work to sing to us young children while supper waited until the men had finished their chores at the barn. She would take Albert on her lap while I sat on a stool by her knee. I have never forgotten the songs that Mother sang. Mothers don't sing any more around the parlor organ or as they go about their work. Is this because the mechanical gadgets do our singing for us, or because our mothers and grandmothers were starved for music?

Our only neighbor was Andy Stevens. His wife surely knew the way to the heart of a small boy. When I was five she was probably 50 years old, but to me she was a very old lady. Why is it that anyone seems old to us, no matter what his age, if he is even 10 years older than we are? One time I challenged this "old" lady to a foot race. She lifted her long skirts off the ground and beat me—to my life-long surprise!

Then there were those great big brown-topped loaves of homemade bread which Mrs. Stevens made. There can never be a sweeter smell than her farm kitchen when she was baking bread, or a more satisfying experience than eating a slice of that bread, fresh from the oven, spread thick with butter and a little brown sugar on top.

Andy Stevens and his wife were perfect examples of millions of self-sufficient farmers who contributed so much to America, but who are now rapidly being overwhelmed and wiped out by the march of so-called progress, with their farms being absorbed and swallowed up by bigger ones.

Their income was small; their wants very few. Andy kept a few cows, a small flock of hens, raised a hog or two, grew an acre or so of potatoes and enough buckwheat for their pancakes. Their diet was simple but ample. Always there were plenty of eggs, milk and butter. The only fresh meat they had was in the fall, when the hogs were butchered. But always, there were delicious hams and bacon, home-cured and smoked in the little smokehouse over burning corn cobs. And, oh yes—there was salt pork the year around.

Like most small farmers, the principal sweet in the Stevens' diet was maple syrup and sugar or molasses and sometimes honey. Yes, Andy Stevens and his wife lived mostly on what they grew, and they sold the small surplus for enough cash to buy a few staple groceries. Yet, somehow, like millions of other small farmers, they raised a family of children, trained in habits of work and responsibility, and sent them forth to take an active part in the leadership of a rapidly developing America.

Where are our young people getting that kind of training now: to walk instead of ride; to feed the calves and the hens every day in the year and to hoe to the end of the row, no matter how long or how hard it is? That was the experience of every farm boy and girl the Day Before Yesterday.

As for Andy himself, I can still see him at the end of the day after long hours of hard work, sitting contentedly, smoking his clay pipe in the corner by the kitchen stove. Back of it was a wood box filled to the brim with wood cut by his own two hands.

Who shall say that Andy's and his wife's contribution is not as important and as great as many of those whose names are on the pages of recorded history. As I think of Andy and his kind, remembered also are lines from Thomas Gray's "Elegy Written in a Country Churchyard."

Oft did the harvest to their sickle yield,
Their furrow oft the stubborn glebe has broke;
How jocund did they drive their team afield!
How bow'd the woods beneath their sturdy stroke!

Let not Ambition mock their useful toil,
Their homely joys, and destiny obscure;
Nor Grandeur hear with a disdainful smile
The short and simple annals of the Poor.

# CHAPTER TWO

# ALWAYS ON THE MOVE

IT WAS MOVING DAY FOR US, AS IT WAS FOR THOU-sands of other rural people, on March 1, 1898. For weeks preceding this time, Father and Mother were absent nearly every day, hunting for a new farm to rent. Finally, near the end of February, they came home one late afternoon showing more enthusiasm than they had in a long time. They had found a place! When we younger boys asked for details, they told us to wait and find out for ourselves.

Then followed an exciting time, packing all the dishes and other breakables in barrels and boxes, and wrapping the furniture, so by the end of the month there wasn't much comfort left in the old house.

Finally, the great day came. My older brother Fay and I were taking a last look, wandering through the empty rooms where we had grown up and been happy. Dashing the tears impatiently from his eyes, Fay ran down the stairs, with me after him, our heavy boots re-echoing through the empty house. Running across the yard, we climbed on the rear end of the big load of furniture. Father spoke to the horses and the load moved down the valley while we watched the old home grow smaller and finally disappear in the distance. Just in this fashion does time change and dim the old chapters as we turn the pages of the new.

Although, by the calendar, the first day of spring had arrived, the weather had not acknowledged the fact. It was bitter cold. The big bobs creaked and squealed as they slid over the dry snow. Trees cracked with the frost, and the pale sun seemed to increase the cold rather than relieve it.

To keep warm, all three of us found it necessary to walk much of the time, swinging and pounding our arms and hands to maintain circulation. Three miles down the valley, we came to a big covered bridge, one of the survivals of the days when timber was plentiful.

"Come on, boys," grumbled Father, "we'll have to carry snow onto those bare bridge planks before we can get across. Get stuck if we don't. I wish the man who invented covered bridges had a 100-year job without pay to keep sleighing on them in the wintertime. Wish I had a dollar for every sleigh load that's been stuck on this bridge!"

"Why did they ever cover bridges, anyway?" asked Fay. "Looks like a waste of timber and work."

"Well, it wasn't. The idea was to protect the timbers of the bridge with the roof, and it *worked*. This bridge has been here since my father's time and it still seems to be sound."

Once across the bridge, it was not far to where the road left the valley for the long pull up the mountain. Here, it was less trouble to keep warm, climbing the long winding hill road, but it was hard going for the horses. There was some ice, and the usual shortness of money in our family had prevented the proper winter shoeing of the horses with sharpened corks.

They were soon puffing and blowing, and it was noon when we reached the summit of the ridge. We paused briefly, blanketed the horses, and fed them some hay from the back of the wagon which Fay had filled before starting. Then we ate some cold sandwiches.

It was much warmer now. The March sun began to give a good account of itself, and hemlocks to the north of us broke some of the cold wind. As Fay turned to look back over the valley from which we had just come, Father said:

"Sort of between two worlds, isn't it?"

To the east and below us stretched the country where we had lived. To the west and below lay the end of our journey and our new home. Over the occasional woods, we could see the winding course of the creek, now covered with ice. A magic blanket of snow glistened and gleamed in the sun with the brilliance of a million diamonds. Smoke flowed from distant farmhouses and bent to the south before the wind. A team and sleigh, looking like a big bug, crawled up the valley road.

"There's the place; there it is!" shouted Father. "Look sharp now—just beyond that clump of trees where the creek crosses the road, you'll see it."

Sure enough, as our gaze followed Father's pointing finger, we could see the little white farmhouse by the bridge and the large barns showing red in the winter

12

*Where do we go from here?* The covered bridge, protected by a roof, was long lived, but the bare floor was poor sleighing in the winter.

sun. Smoke rose from the chimney. There was home. Mother was already there, settling the first load of goods which had been moved over the mountain the day before.

I have often wished I could put into words the feelings of a 13-year-old boy. Everything was new and different, both in the neighborhood and on the farm. For the few years just preceding, we had lived on a small place. The new farm was large. There was a big dairy and several hundred hens—a large flock for those days. The neighborhood itself was five miles over a mountain from the nearest railroad and village. Public transportation was by a stagecoach that went down the valley in the early morning, carrying passengers and some small freight. If a housewife was unable to get to the village once a week to do her few errands, the stage driver did them for her at the big village at the end of the line. When the driver returned up the valley at close of day, he delivered the mail to a farm kitchen that served as the neighborhood post office. There were, of course, no modern gadgets for communication or travel such as those we have today. Almost all of our world was confined to the neighborhood, the country church, the one-room school, and especially our farm. So our world was limited, but it was enough. I can remember no other period of my life when I was happier than in 1898, when I was 13 years old. For the first time—on that big farm—I was given definite chores to do, and I had to assume the responsibility for them. It was my job to milk five or six of the cows, out of the large herd, every night and morning.

Spring was opening up and I was expected to help tap the maple grove and boil the maple sap into syrup and sugar. Later, I helped plant by hand the garden of corn and potatoes. In short, aside from attending the district school, I took pride in keeping up with the men, trying always to milk more cows, hoe more corn and potatoes, and do more work than they did.

One of the pleasant jobs that stands out in memory the spring when we moved was the gathering of the eggs. At the close of day, it was my job to go through the long henhouse with a large pail or basket and pick the eggs from the nests where sometimes there might be eight or ten in the same nest. When I came out of that henhouse, perhaps carrying two large full pails of eggs, I had the feeling a prospector for gold must have when he strikes it rich!

However, there was an episode somewhat related to that henhouse that is not quite so pleasant to remember. I got the idea somewhere that a balloon could be made to go up by inflating it with hot air. So I stole one of Mother's big flour sacks, sneaked a kerosene light out of the house, and set up operations too near the henhouse. I put the lighted lamp under the mouth of the flour sack, and with stones weighted the edges of the sack as tightly as I could to the ground. Then I waited for the sack to inflate when, according to my notion, I could remove the stones and the sack would sail away. But alas, as Robert Burns wrote: "The best laid schemes o' mice and men Gang aft a-gley."

Instead of sailing into the air as a balloon should, the darn sack caught fire, set the dry grass near the henhouse afire, and then started on the building itself. My yells brought help and water from the house, and the fire was soon put out. Let's not dwell on the slight unpleasantness which followed!

\* \* \*

If you have never had to move when you were young, you missed the excitement of exploring the house that is to be your new home. I remember how my young brother and I rushed from one room to another, before much of our furniture was moved in, to see what each room was like and to try to figure which one would be ours. In one upper chamber, piled high, was a great store of books and magazines purposely left by the former owner because he had no way to carry them to the distant home to which he was moving. Because the new house was large, we didn't settle that room but left the books just as they were. What a joy it was to us boys, whose chief recreation was reading, to sit in that room by the hour—completely absorbed, completely lost—with those books and magazines!

In our new neighborhood, there was a family whose lease had expired on March 1. They had been unable to rent a new farm, however, so that they didn't move out, but were there when the new tenants with their furniture appeared. There followed some arguments between the old and the new tenants; but since the old tenants had no place to go and the new ones did not want to turn the family out into the road in the March blizzards, they all moved in together. The new tenants unloaded most of their furniture in the barn

15

and spread their mattresses at night on the kitchen floor. They lived that way for several weeks until the old tenants finally found a new place to live. They parted the best of friends.

I like to remember that incident as an example of how both individuals and nations *can* settle their difficulties if they are willing to give and take, if they are men of good will.

Until my parents finally bought a farm, we moved frequently, always on March 1. My job has made it necessary for Belle and me to move many times. One of my dreams is to have the privilege of going back to the many houses in which I have lived as boy and man and exploring every room again. What memories of sorrow and joy they would recall!

\* \* \*

I had a friend whose great-grandmother married in Connecticut. With an ox-team and a few cherished possessions, she and her husband left their home to build a new one in the wilderness of central New York. Before they disappeared into a forest, the couple stopped at the crest of a hill to turn and look back on the pleasant home and valley they had just left. They well knew that when they turned their backs to resume their journey, the chances were they would never again see their old homes or their loved ones on this earth.

After weeks of following the rough trail that led through the forest and fording the various streams, the couple came at long last to the spot where the husband had decided they were to build their new home.

My friend told me the family story of how the young bride nearly died of homesickness during those first few months in their little cabin in the wilderness. Back of the cabin in a cleared space, there was a huge rock very similar to the many with which the girl was familiar near her old home. Sometimes when her lonesomeness became almost unbearable, she would go out and climb on that rock. Somehow, the solid firmness of the rock seemed to comfort her. Then, after a time, the babies began to come and the work of the pioneer woman increased. Her husband was good to her, so the pain was replaced by just a general sadness when she thought of her old home.

How many, many times in our history that story has been duplicated. How many, many times the hearts of both the father and mother have been torn by the death of their babies and children because it was so difficult in pioneer times to give them the medical care they needed.

As you read the stories, or look at them on television, of the trek westward by oxcart, sleigh, or covered wagon, you may not realize the tremendous courage it took to make those long, slow journeys and to endure the hardships and sadness. No wonder they danced and sang and told stories around the camp fires! They did it to build their courage and to keep the lumps out of their throats and the tears out of their eyes.

From the time of the first settlements, Americans have been movers; so much so, that it is difficult to find century farmers—people whose families have stayed put and lived on the same farm for at least 100 years. This restless pioneer spirit in most of us— always trying to better our lot—made America as we know it today. I often think, as I am sure you have, of the limitless courage, particularly of the women, who left almost everything and everybody behind, piled their few possessions onto a sleigh or wagon, and moved into a strange country or neighborhood. It is not hard to realize how difficult it was for a woman to have anything nice after it has been moved several times on a wagon or sleigh, or in boxcars the way our furniture was moved before the days of trucks and modern moving vans.

I must add that, out of the innumerable times that either my parents or my wife and I have moved, I never heard a single complaint from the women. Without their help, encouragement, and faith, America could never have been settled.

# CHAPTER THREE

# NEIGHBORS—CANTANKEROUS AND OTHERWISE

OUR NEIGHBOR, MR. RICHARDSON, WAS A GOOD man, but he was very big and fat. I remember how scared I was one day when he fell in our yard and couldn't get up. Father sent us on the run for a neighbor to help him get Mr. Richardson on his feet. Once up, he seemed able to navigate again. I have always remembered Mr. Richardson, because he gave me just about the most interesting experience that a small boy growing up Day Before Yesterday could have. He invited me to go with him to the county seat, a town of 3000 or 4000 people, which was about 10 miles away from home. I had never been there. How that buggy settled to one side after Mr. Richardson, with considerable difficulty, got into it. There

18

was not much room left for me on the narrow buggy seat, but what's a little discomfort when one is going on a big adventure?

Down the valley road we went, arriving after a while in Owego, only a large country town, but it seemed like a big city to me. Putting the horse into the livery stable, we went across the road to get our dinner—my first meal in a public eating place. By the way, the noon meal was called dinner and supper was at night. None of this new-fangled idea of lunch at noon and dinner at night; or skipping breakfast and combining lunch with a mid-morning snack and calling it brunch.

Now it has been my fortune, or misfortune, to eat in many and diverse places in cities and country, in restaurants and in homes, but not one of them stands out in my memory like that dinner in the Dugan House with Mr. Richardson. Remember how those old-time hotel tables were set? In the center was a revolving caster with slots in it for bottles holding among other things vinegar, pepper sauce, and catsup. Except for the dessert, you were never asked what you wanted to eat. It was all piled on the table at one time in such variety and profusion that you were

sorry you couldn't eat enough to last a week. And what do you think Mr. Richardson paid for that meal? Twenty-five cents apiece!

\* \* \*

Mr. John, neighbor for whom I worked by the day, put from 10 to 20 barrels of cider into his cellar every fall, the number depending on the size of his apple crop; but whatever the number, there was never enough. Sometimes, when life got a little complicated or too tough for him, he tried to neutralize the situation with more than his usual allotment of his favorite beverage.

What little mail Mr. John and the rest of us in the neighborhood received came up the valley each day by stagecoach from the county seat, and was delivered to a farm home where the kitchen served as the local post office. This country post office was about a half mile from Mr. John's home, and to get there, one had to cross a narrow, swinging footbridge over a creek.

At the close of a summer's day, I was milking in Mr. John's stable close to the creek when, feeling less pain than usual, he announced that I could milk the rest of the cows while he went after the mail. Then he made his uncertain way down the long stable and out the door. Soon after, I heard a great yell followed by a loud splash. Rushing to the door of the stable I saw Mr. John crawling up the bank of the creek quite sober, also quite mad, looking like the setting hens we used to duck in the watering trough to make them stop trying to raise a family and get back to laying eggs.

But while Mr. John sometimes overdid the hard cider, make no mistake about his real worth. The judgment of a boy about a man for whom he works is likely to be an accurate one. The winter I helped Mr. John with the chores was a bitterly cold one, and he never permitted me to get out of bed until he had had time to build a roaring fire in the kitchen range, where I could dress before going out in the dark cold morning.

When working for Mr. John in the fields with other men, he watched out to see that I didn't overdo and often gave me the easier jobs. Those are the things a boy never forgets.

\* \* \*

My Uncle Mark Roe, all dressed up in his Sunday-go-to-meetin' clothes.

I once knew a fellow whose name was Angell, but, God rest his soul, *he was no angel*. Now I don't know whether there's any connection between red hair and temper or not, but Mr. Angell was red-headed. He owned—at least on paper—and operated a small butter-and-milk factory where my folks delivered the milk in 1898. Almost daily, Mr. Angell and his poor worn-out old stationary engine staged a fight, and it was always an open question as to who was going to win. While the argument was going on, farmers would stand around, waiting to unload their milk, but the delay was usually worthwhile because the fireworks were so interesting. After considerable tinkering, coaxing, and especially swearing. Mr. Angell's engine usually would consent to resume operations and all would be well again temporarily.

One bright June morning when milk deliveries were at the high point of the year, the engine balked again, and in spite of all Mr. Angell's work and swearing, it just would not start. All of us who had come to deliver our milk stood around and watched. Suddenly, Mr. Angell came absolutely to the end of his rope or patience. Grabbing a heavy maul, he rocked the old engine on its foundation, finally driving a hole in the boiler so that the escaping steam chased him and the rest of us to a safe distance.

There he was, with probably 50 or 60 40-quart cans of milk all ready to separate and no way under the sun to do it. He had to pay us for the milk, which we took home to feed what we could of it to the stock. The fit of temper probably put Mr. Angell into bankruptcy. He got in his buggy, drove 10 miles to Owego, hired a mechanical engineer at the un-heard of price of $5 a day, and got the old engine eventually to totter along on its way again. But not for long. Mr. Angell soon closed the factory and our market for milk, and moved to California, where I hope he found life more serene and agreeable—but probably didn't, because serenity comes from our own hearts.

\* \* \*

Neighbor Elston was a bore. Like all bores, he loved to talk on and on, saying nothing. Because of his natural courtesy and his dislike of hurting any-one's feelings, Father was Mr. Elston's captive audi-ence. On rainy days, on Sundays, and other times when he thought Father would not be at work, Elston would come meandering down the road for a visit. Father's favorite resting place was a corner of the big bay window, which was mostly filled with Mother's house plants. I can close my eyes even now and see Father gently rocking back and forth in a Boston rocker with one foot caught behind the other while he read a book or magazine.

On many such occasions, Father would look up to see Elston coming down the road, all set to ruin a good two hours of Father's time. When he saw Elston coming, Father would always jump to his feet in a rage, slam his book or magazine on the floor, and shout, "There comes that damned old fool again!" But by the time Elston had come up the walk to the stoop, Father would be right out there, his hand extended, with a welcoming smile on his face and saying:

"Why, hello there. I'm so glad to see you. Come right in, come right in."

That same neighbor, Elston, had a feud with a neighbor named Brinkley, which ran on for 40 years or more. The quarrel was over a line fence and it involved not more than a few feet of land, probably not worth $5. Why it was that line fences were such a perennial cause of argument between neighbors,

I'll never know! For example, I knew a couple of rural neighbors once whose houses were close together. Between them was a tight board fence at least 10 feet high. On one side of the fence, in big letters, was painted the sentence: "My *neighbor* built this fence."

Well, Mr. Elston and Mr. Brinkley had not spoken to each other for many years. Their quarrel was a nuisance in the neighborhood because there were times when it was necessary for neighbors to change work and cooperate in many other ways.

My older brother was irritated with the quarrel because he wanted to get these two nearest neighbors to change off with him in delivering milk to the butter factory. So my brother got the bright idea that he could act as peacemaker. He almost succeeded— but not quite. He got Mr. Elston and Mr. Brinkley to walk out to the line fence together in order to try to agree where the line should be. At one place, the line crossed the creek. When they came to the edge of the creek, Mr. Elston hesitated to walk through it with his shoes on, so Mr. Brinkley, who had on rubber boots, took Elston on his back and they started across. Afterwards, my brother always lamented the fact that he didn't have a picture of what happened.

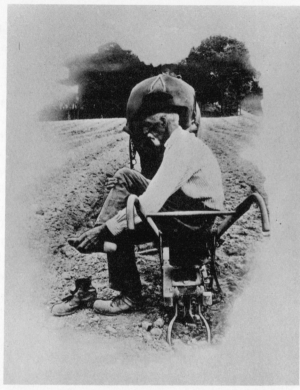

Many a day I have followed a horse and cultivator back and forth, back and forth across a corn or potato field, stopping once in a while just like this old fellow to take the stones and dirt out of my shoes and rest my feet.

When they got into the middle of the creek, the quarrel broke out afresh and Brinkley dumped Elston off his back and into the water. Then he stormed home. After that, the quarrel went on until they died. For all I know it may be going on still!

Old-timers will remember when the country roads were "worked" or repaired every spring through the cooperation of the neighbors, all of whom saved paying their road taxes in cash by contributing both man and horsepower. The work in each neighborhood was supervised by some farmer who had been elected to the office of pathmaster. Often, the pathmaster didn't know any more about making a good road than the man in the moon. If you have ever driven on one of those roads rounded up in the middle by sod, mud, and stones, you will know what I mean. Nevertheless, the pathmasters thought they knew how, and some of them liked to throw their weight around by being the "big boss."

Among these was Mr. Elston. So, early one spring morning after he had been elected pathmaster—probably because no one else would take the job—he thought to himself that there was an opportunity to show Brinkley who was boss around these parts. So

23

he stalked over into Brinkley's yard and ordered him in no uncertain language to get off his hind-end, get out his team, and join with the other neighbors to work out his road tax. Brinkley, who was six feet tall, took one look at his cocky little neighbor, grabbed a neck yoke, and took after Elston. Then ensued a foot race that might have ended in a funeral if Elston had not been able to outrun his enemy.

Yet Mr. Brinkley was really kind at heart. His wife had died, his children had grown and gone, so he lived alone. Feeling sorry for him, my mother frequently used to take him a fresh loaf of homemade bread, or maybe a pie or a cake. He worked his farm with only a little extra help at haying time, and sometimes, when I was a boy, I was that extra help. I like to think of Mr. Brinkley stopping to lean on his fork when pitching hay on the wagon for me to load, while I eased my tired muscles and he his lonely soul by visiting. He talked to me about things he had thought about in the long hours that he spent alone. Invariably, he would start his sentences with, "Says I to myself, says I."

\* \* \*

There comes to mind an elderly gentleman who visited my home regularly when I was a boy. He was a justice of the peace, and came every three months to have Father swear to an affidavit in order to draw his small Civil War pension. For his long trip to our home and for his services, the old man received the magnificent sum of 25 cents. That was all he ever asked. On his head, he always wore a tall stovepipe hat, which, in spite of its very apparent age, gave great dignity to this gentleman of the old school. When ready for business, he would sit at the kitchen table, lay his hat on it, bottom-side up, and out of it take the papers needed for the transaction. Many times since, when scribbling rapidly with a pen, I have remembered the great care with which this old gentleman poised his pen for a moment, over what he was going to write, and then wrote it in a script which was easier to read than print.

\* \* \*

One late June day when I was young, I took a big pail and went across the valley and up a long hill to pick wild strawberries. I was lucky enough to find that paradise of a berry picker's heart—an old meadow

24

where the ground was almost red with berries. So far was I from any human habitation that, with one exception, the quiet was broken only by the hum of insects and the song of the birds. The exception was a farmer plowing a short distance above me on the hillside and shouting at his team.

The farmer was Mr. Melden, a good example of what we used to call "buckwheat farmers." They were the ones who were too lazy or maybe too interested in things other than farming ever to get around to plant their crops when they should be planted. So they planted buckwheat, which didn't have to be sown until around the first of July.

It disturbed me to know that Mr. Melden was plowing under just about the best lot of strawberries that I had ever seen. But my irritation was softened with amusement because of the language Melden used in order to get a little work out of the "crowbaits" which he used for a team. I wish there was some way to put on paper "the words and the music" that Melden used to cuss his team without using a real swear word. He could say, "Gingers to grindstones, gol darn ye, gosh all beeswax, Molly, you get your ill-begotten carcass out of that furrow or I'll break every bone in your dad-blamed body" with emphasis and spirit that beat any real cussin' I ever heard.

Poor Mr. Melden! His wife, who had the reputation in the neighborhood of being a nagger, and his unsuccessful attempts at farming, finally became just too much for him. One morning, he came up missing in the neighborhood. Long years afterwards, there was an unconfirmed report that Melden had "escaped" to Alaska, struck it rich, and raised another family. Maybe he wasn't as old as I thought he was when I was a boy!

\* \* \*

I have often wondered about the many men and women whom my mother helped into the world, either with or without the assistance of a doctor. Seldom was there a birth in our own neighborhood when Mother was not called upon to help. Often we had to get our own breakfast because Mother had been sent for in the night.

Where are those men and women now who first saw the light when Mother was there? Have their lives justified their living?

\* \* \*

25

Delivering milk to the milk station or creamery was a daily chore. That was why it was necessary for neighbors to take turns or "change works" with one another in order to do it.

When Father died and the family was broken up, Mother moved to a little house in the nearby village. In that neighborhood there lived (and still does at this writing) a florist by the name of William Stimming. As a young man, Bill had taken over a very small greenhouse business, finally building it into a wholesale business known throughout the eastern states.

In addition to building a great business, Bill has always had time to be just about the best neighbor— in the true sense of the word—that I have known. Bill is active both locally and state-wide in the leadership of his church, in the Boy Scouts, in education, and many other public activities. But best of all, he has gladdened the hearts of hundreds of people by the generous distribution of his "weeds," as he calls his flowers. Seldom is there a sad or joyous occasion for miles around that is not graced by Bill's flowers.

For many years, when Mother lived alone, often when she opened her door in the morning to get her little bottle of milk, her day and her heart would be gladdened by a beautiful bouquet of Bill Stimming's "weeds."

\* \* \*

One of my brothers, then married and operating a little farm of his own, was taken very ill right at the beginning of haying time. Worry about getting his haying done retarded his recovery, so one morning when he looked from his bedroom window across his big unmowed meadow, he saw 17 of his neighbors with their teams and mowing machines cutting his grass. When it was dry, they came again and put it into the barn.

Among those who took part in that haying bee for my brother was a Polish neighbor, Mr. Z. He left his team hitched to his mowing machine for a moment to go into the kitchen to get a drink of water. With the dipper of water in his hand, he looked up just in time to see his team starting on a run out of the yard and down the road. Dropping the dipper of water with a loud splash on the kitchen floor, Mr. Z dashed after his runaway team. In the meantime, another neighbor, standing by, seeing what was happening, yelled, "Whoa, Whoa" at the horses, but they didn't understand the term because Mr. Z had taught them to obey "Stop! Stop!" The horses ended up by their home barn, unharmed, but the mowing machine was ruined.

Testifying to the affection which Mr. Z's neighbors had for him was the fact that a few days after his team had run away, ruining his mowing machine, a spokesman for the neighbors handed him a sum of money with which to buy a new machine.

But Mr. Z found it difficult to farm here in America, where our practices are so different from what he had been used to in Poland. During one haying time, he borrowed my brother's big lumber wagon with his hay rigging. Now my brother had warned him several times that when coming down his steep hill with a load of hay, he should chain a wheel to act as a brake. Don, my oldest son, was staying with my brother that summer, and on that particular day was helping Mr. Z with his haying. When Don got back to my brother's that night, he said, "Uncle, Mr. Z's hay load got out of control. The horses ran away down the hill, smashing the wagon in the fence."

"Good!" said my brother, "I've *told* that darned old fool to chain the wheel on that hill."

Don hesitated for a moment before adding, "Yes, Uncle, but it was *your* wagon!"

Many times I have remembered that incident and thought how quickly our point of view can change when it is *our* wagon.

\* \* \*

At the turn of the century and with the coming of the automobile, farming and living in country neighborhoods were not much different from what they had been in the days of the first settlements. To those of us who are old enough to remember the horse-and-buggy days, the changes since are almost unbelievable.

Country communities were largely sufficient unto themselves. The farmer grew most of his own food. He went to the nearest village on Saturday afternoons for the few staple groceries and farm supplies he needed, and those trips provided his amusement, for such contraptions as the phonograph, radio, automobile, and television were beyond imagination.

There was not, at that time, a single telephone in the whole neighborhood.

Such a community was Michigan Hill (with the accent on the last syllable), near Richford, New York, in the extreme northern part of Tioga, a southern tier county. Legend has it that Michigan Hill was settled by some pioneers who were headed west, but who became tired and discouraged and settled on that high hill, which they named Michigan. For 100 years after the first settlement there, Michigan Hill was a thriving, typical American community, sending forth its surplus of boys and girls to make their way in the outside world.

Among those born there was John D. Rockefeller, Sr., the oil king who became one of the richest men in the world.

Because Belle, my wife, is a Rockefeller, from another branch of the family, we frequently go back to the Hill for a picnic where so many of our Rockefeller relatives once lived. But it's always a little saddening, for, like so many farm communities, except for a few isolated farms, Michigan Hill is largely deserted, grown to brush, and the buildings gone or fallen into ruin.

28

Like me, John D. Rockefeller in his later years used to like to return frequently to the scene of his birthplace—or "borning ground." On one such occasion, years ago, he stopped at the little village store to inquire about the condition of the dirt road that led up to Michigan Hill. An old gentleman of whom everyone was very fond was prompt in speaking up.

"I was born up there and I'll be glad to show you the way."

John D. answered, "I know the way, but come along with me and my party."

So they all rode up and over the hill with the old man, pointing out who had once lived here and there. When they came to the deserted house where John D. was born, the old gentleman explained in detail that *this* was the place where John D. Rockefeller first saw the light of day. Then he went on to tell that the house was now owned by Simeon Rockefeller's widow. In due time, the party came back to the little village grocery store and the guide got out of the car. John D. thanked him and then added kindly, "*I* am John D. Rockefeller." All the rest of his life the old man never ceased to talk about his wonderful adventure.

Although I have heard them many times, I never tire of the folklore stories about the people of Michigan Hill who lived Day Before Yesterday and who were so typical of the thousands of country people of their times.

There is a story of Belle's Uncle, Simeon Rockefeller, who answered Abe Lincoln's call for volunteers and, like thousands of other boys both North and South, went away to war. A sad and lonesome time passed, until finally word came back that Simeon was dead. Memorial services were held for him in the church in the valley. More dreary time passed until one day, Simeon's mother, who was working in her kitchen, happened to look up and see her son making his slow and painful way across the lot to his home. He had been very ill. You can imagine the joy of that mother when she saw her son returned from the dead.

On Michigan Hill, there lived a couple known as Eben and Pamela, who were coming back to the Hill one cold winter day from the little village. They were riding in a "longsleigh" packed with their robes and soap stones to keep them warm, groceries, and milk cans full of skim milk. The road was badly

Working out the road taxes. The neighbors came early in the spring with teams, roadscraper, rakes and shovels to repair the dirt roads. The boss, also a neighbor, was called the path-master.

drifted, and when they tried to get through one of the snowdrifts, the sleigh tipped over. Pamela was packed beneath the supplies with a milk can and various and sundry packages on top of her. Very deliberately, Eben went about setting things to rights while Pamela kept yelling, "Eben, Eben, help me out!" And as he went on about his business, he said, "I will, I will." He righted the supplies, straightened out his tangled team, picked up all the milk cans,

while all the time Pamela kept calling to him to help her out. Finally, after everything else in the sleigh was set right and ready to go, Eben pulled the milk can and the rest of the things off Pamela and helped her into the sleigh. What do you suppose she said to him then?

Another old Michigan Hill story is about the local character who didn't have all his "buttons," and some local wag told this fellow (whom we will call Enoch)

30

that Old Lady Hall, up the road a-ways, would buy a woodchuck skin from him to use as a nightcap. So Enoch went hunting for a woodchuck, got one, skinned it and hung the hide up to dry. After two or three hot summer days when the skin was good and "ripe," Enoch took it to Mrs. Hall.

"What do I want with that thing?" she asked.

"You want it for a nightcap, and I want my pay," Enoch told her.

A brief but violent argument followed, which ended with Enoch shouting at the woman.

"You damned old fool. You don't know what you do want." Then he threw the skin at her feet and went away.

One time, my wife's Aunt had some paste all ready to paper a room. (They did their own papering in those days.) When her back was turned for a few minutes, Enoch ate up the whole pan of paste, after which he told her. "That was good puddin' but t'would have been better if you'd remembered the sweetnin'."

I like the story about my wife's Grandfather Rockefeller, who lived a mile or so up a long hill from the little neighborhood schoolhouse. One bad, stormy night, he set out with his dog to go to the weekly prayer meeting. Upon his return, Grandmother Rockefeller asked him, "How many were there?" To this he replied, "Three—God, my dog, and me."

Within a stone's throw of the old Rockefeller homestead where John D. was born, is the dilapidated schoolhouse which served as a school, a church, and the community center for the whole neighborhood.

A regular attendant at Sunday and prayer meetings held in the schoolhouse was a prominent citizen in the neighborhood who always chewed a small cud of tobacco; and when he rose to "testify," he was in the habit of removing his cud from his mouth and putting it carefully on the seat beside him. Knowing this, one of the boys, urged on by others, sat beside the gentleman at one of the prayer meetings. When he had the opportunity, he removed the cud of tobacco from the seat and replaced it with a small wad of tansy. Although this is a true story, I never learned just what happened when the man put that tansy into his mouth. But knowing how bitter it tastes, I can imagine that the gentleman probably would have lost all of his Christian principles if he could have laid hands on those boys.

In that schoolhouse the folks met for spelling matches, for singing, debates, and long talks, for church and Sunday school services and for prayer meeting every Thursday night. Once in a while, there would be a good, old-fashioned rousing revival meeting at which a good part of the community got religion—from which, unfortunately, many recovered soon afterwards. And finally, when some lifelong neighbor came to the end of his road, the whole neighborhood gathered round in that little schoolhouse to listen to a funeral sermon and pay respect to the one they had loved and with whom they had quarreled, worked, and prayed.

* * *

So it was with the neighbors and the neighborhoods Day Before Yesterday. The neighbors represented a cross-section of human nature. Everything else in the world can change, but human nature never does. The neighbors could be—and sometimes were—disagreeable and cantankerous to the point of meanness. Boy, how they could gossip! And like members of your own family, how they could criticize one another. Nevertheless, again like members of your family, let one of them burn out with a fire, get sick or have some other trouble, and his fellow neighbors, never failed to rally round. They couldn't do enough.

The neighborhoods were sufficient unto themselves. Over the hill was a strange country, inhabited by strange people. Then came the automobile and *change!* Instead of evening meetings and social affairs in the home, the little red schoolhouse or the country church, the car made it possible to have countywide and even statewide meetings almost as easily attended as were the old-time local meetings.

Were the lives of the older people I knew **Day Before Yesterday** worthwhile? Did most of them make a contribution? Did they "pay their passage"? Most of them did, I know. There was an Italian family who lived near Mother in her later years. With hard work and America's golden opportunities, the father and mother helped every one of their children to help themselves to get an education. Every one of the children was brought up to work. One of the children became an outstanding physician.

Nearly every one of the children entered the world with Mother's help. All of them made good citizens. One does not have to be famous to be truly great. As I look back on the lives of the men and women I knew in Father's generation, I know that the great majority of them were good people, excellent citizens, and good neighbors.

I used to dream and say in public talks that the great changes in communication and transportation had the possibilities of making the whole world one neighborhood, of clearing up misunderstandings, and making us all friends and neighbors. But it has not worked that way. Maybe we have expected too much in too short a time.

Maybe we can still cling to the hope that sometime, the ever-increasing facilities for better understanding among the people of the world will make all of us "God's chilluns"—neighbors and friends.

# CHAPTER FOUR

# GOING TO THE FAIR

Country and village boys and girls did not get to celebrate many holidays Day Before Yesterday.

One of the hottest and hardest working days I remember was a Fourth of July spent in a hayfield. Sometimes, on the evening of the Fourth, we would shoot off a nickel pack of fire-crackers. On May 30, we took time off to attend the Decoration Day exercises and the parade from the village to the cemetery when the old soldiers were still able to march or ride at the head of the column.

Mother always worked for days preparing the big dinner for Thanksgiving Day, and she did the same at Christmas. We observed Christmas by hanging our stockings on the mantle, happy if we found in them on Christmas morning a big Florida sweet orange, a long stick of striped candy, and maybe a single inexpensive toy or doll under the stocking on the floor.

So it is hard for the sophisticated boys and girls of today, who have gone everywhere and have everything, to understand how few holidays and how little of the material things most of their grandfathers and grandmothers had. But I doubt if modern children are any happier than we were. What you don't have, you don't miss, and when you have but little, you are very appreciative of what you do have.

But there was one holiday that we celebrated every year. That was the day we attended the county agricultural fair! There was no oversleeping on the morning of that big day. We got up an hour earlier than usual. Father and we boys hurried through the chores while the last squawk of the luckless rooster showed the preparations of the women for the picnic luncheon. How the roosters of those days must have cursed those farm holidays.

When the chores were done, breakfast eaten, and the lunch packed, like nearly everyone else in the neighborhood, we started for the fairgrounds. Although the automobile had just started to come around, almost everybody rode behind farm work horses. The degree of prosperity of the family was indicated by the quality of their horses and the vehicles in which they rode. There were, of course, the buggies which the boys had carefully washed and greased. Sometimes they forgot to grease them and were reminded of that mistake when the axles began to squeal on the way to the fair, to the vast amusement of everyone except the family in the wagon.

How proud a neighbor was who had a horse that was a pacer. There was no jerking of the dog-cart or any other vehicle drawn by a pacer.

In addition to the buggies, there was in the procession just about every other farm conveyance—good, bad, and indifferent.

Out of the hills and valleys, they came. A long stream of humanity from every direction, headed toward the fairgrounds. Over the parade arose a great thick cloud of dust, not unlike the smoke of a long line of battle, covering clothes, and filling noses, mouths, and eyes. But what did we care? What did a little thing like dust matter? We were going to the fair—seeking some relaxation and fun, as a thirsty man seeks water.

When we came to the entrance gate that led through the high, tight board fence that enclosed the fairgrounds, I could hear the organ on the merry-go-round playing "In the Good Old Summertime," a very popular new tune at the time. On rare occasions when I hear it played on radio or television today, it takes me back 50 years or more to that organ grinding out the tune on the rapidly moving merry-go-round.

Mixed with the music were the shouting of the side-show barkers and all the other noises of a fair in progress.

How impatient I was with Father because he seemed so slow in buying the tickets so that we could get into paradise. But my eagerness and anticipation were cooled a bit when I saw a man with a badge—a constable—leading a boy of about my age out of the gate. Father said that the boy had tried to crawl under the fairground fence instead of paying his fare and got caught at it. I felt sorry for him, for I knew how hard it was to get the 25 cents necessary to buy a boy's ticket.

When we were inside, I thought we would never get around the other wagons and the crowd so that we could drive way down to the back of the fairgrounds where we could hitch our horses. But after what seemed to be an eternity, we finally got back up to the racetrack just in time to see and hear members of the village band in their brand-new uniforms and with their shiny instruments gleaming in the morning sunshine, marching up the track toward their place in the bandstand. Just as the band got in front of me, as I stood by the fence that guarded the track, there was a preliminary roll of the snare drum and the band broke into the stirring strains of the "Stars and Stripes Forever," written by the great march king, John Philip Sousa, to honor the soldiers of the Spanish-American War. To me, and probably to most others, there is something elemental that stirs my heart when I see a body of marching men and hear the insistent and powerful call of the drum.

I pretty nearly busted with pride when I saw my oldest brother, Charlie, resplendent in his brand-new uniform. How eagerly and intently I listened for and heard the shrill notes of his clarinet as, with head up and shoulders erect, he marched with the others in the village band.

Charlie died not long afterwards, and in the long years since, I have often thought of him marching and playing the clarinet in time with the big brass drum:

Come, come, come along with me
Come, come, come along with me
Leave that earthy body of yours
And all material things, and
Come with me to the Land of Dreams,
To the Land of Spirit, to the Land
Of Beauty, exaltation and happiness
Where all things are right.

When the band reached its stand, it was time to go to the ball game. Now, you may be a modern baseball fan, as I am, and watch every big league game that you can, but if you never attended a baseball game between the teams of two neighboring villages 50 years ago, you have never seen a real ball game.

This beautiful young Percheron bred by Darwin Rumsey and his son, Fred, was exhibited at the Tompkins county fair in 1887.

37

In the first place, we knew every man on our own local team, so that we were bitterly partisan for our own boys. The crowd was so close to the base lines that the local constable couldn't prevent masses of people from surging onto the diamond and taking part in an argument when there was one—which occurred in practically every inning. And God help the umpire! There never was but one, and how he ever survived the rows which usually centered around him, I'll never know. About the only peace that prevailed during the entire game was when the boys lost a ball and all hands joined to help find it. Those old-time boys could play ball. I have seen some games with low scores played by town teams that were just as good as those played by professionals today.

\* \* \*

Of course, to many of those who went to the agricultural fairs, the day wasn't complete without attending the horse and trotting races. But it is not necessary to describe them here, for they are one of the few things that have not greatly changed over the years. I liked the horse races better than I did the trotting, until that day when I was standing beside the

track near one of the entrance gates farthest from the grandstand. As the horses galloped by, their riders bending low over their necks, the saddle girth broke or became loose on one, throwing the rider. But as he went off the horse, his foot caught in the stirrup. Pulled by the sideway drag of the man's body, the horse turned and went through the gate beside me. As they went through, the man's head hit the post with a sickening thud. Horrified, I ran through the gate after the horse and man. A few rods down the highway, the man's foot was released and he was left in the dusty road while the horse galloped away. I was the first person to get to the man, and although I had never seen a dead man before, I knew that this one would never ride again.

\* \* \*

In this space age, when flying is as common as railroad travel used to be, and when we are even planning to go to the moon, no one can appreciate now how thrilled everyone was at the balloon ascension at the county fair. It topped all the other events. Time after time during the day, I left whatever I was watching to run across the racetrack to see how rapidly the big balloon was filling with gas. Finally, it went up, while our hearts almost stood still to see the aerialist hang by his knees on the trapeze, or perform other daredevil acts. We stretched our necks and strained our eyes until the ballon became a speck in the distant sky and finally disappeared. The next day, the memories of our wonderful time at the fair were saddened when we heard that something had gone wrong when the balloonist tried to land and that he had been killed.

*  *  *

No day at the old-time country fair was complete unless you took time off to look at the agricultural and homemaking exhibits; and if you were a farmer, you couldn't help but be at least a little proud of your occupation. Exhibits of beautiful cattle and the products of farm and garden set the goal of perfection for the whole community. The exhibits and the inspiration to do an even better job of production were the real reasons for the fair's existence, although a day off for recreation and entertainment was also good, of course. But today, too many fairs have lost sight of the real purpose of an agricultural fair and are taking the taxpayers' money for too much and too many unwholesome midway attractions.

One time, Father had a winter squash vine in his garden that, early in the season, seemed to be a bit unusual. So he began taking care of the squash as if it were his youngest child. I don't know if it did any good, but he fed the growing vine with copious applications of skim milk, and, like Jack's beanstalk, that squash grew and grew until by fair time, it looked like the grandfather of all squashes. So Father put it on exhibit at the fair and when he won a blue ribbon, he bragged about it for weeks afterward.

*  *  *

There was one attraction at the fair that I always liked to watch with mixed feelings of envy and admiration until I got a girl myself—that was, to see a young couple all dressed in their best clothes, walking hand in hand, having the time of their lives not only because of the attractions of the fair but because of each other. Often, each would be carrying in a free hand a big stick of spun candy. If, mayhap, they got an opportunity to sneak a kiss, it must have been sort of sticky.

* * *

Finally, the big day came to an end and we rode home filled with pleasant memories that have lasted a lifetime. But one day a year at the fair was enough!

No hard, long day in the hayfield ever made me so tired as it did to walk around the fairgrounds in a hot winter suit, the only one I had.

How good it was to get back home at night and get those "Sunday go-to-meetin'" clothes off and pull on the cool overalls and shirt and go down to the barn to help with the milking.

# CHAPTER FIVE

# IN A
# BLACKBERRY PATCH

Come on," said my father. "Stir yourself, we're going blackberrying."

Some people like to fish, some like to hunt, but ever since I was a small boy there has never been anything out-of-doors that I liked better than picking berries.

But before this particular morning it had rained all night, and I knew the grass and bushes would be sopping wet. So I objected, telling Father that it was no day to go after berries. But he said that the weather would soon clear and that the bushes would be dry by the time we got to them.

Pointing to a little patch of blue sky on the northwest horizon, Father said, "In this climate, when you see blue sky in the West or Northwest, especially when the wind blows from that direction, you can be pretty sure that it will be a nice day. But a south wind usually means more rain."

"Look," he added, "what little fog there is is settling, not climbing the hill, for there is truth in the old saying:

'When the fog goes up the hill
There will be water for the mill.' "

Still in an argumentative mood, I said, "Yeah, but Mother said this morning when she was getting breakfast that water boiled away in the tea kettle almost faster than she could put it in. Doesn't that mean rain?"

"That's enough argument," snapped Father. "Get your pails and let's get started."

Each of us took a 16-quart milk pail to carry the berries and a small 2-quart pail which we hung by a strap around our waists so as to have both hands free with which to pick the berries. We climbed a long ridge on the back of our farm and then walked through the fields along the plateau on top, some three miles to the big slashing where the blackberries grew. Of course, we had not gone far before our feet

and legs were wet to the knees from walking through the high grass. But farm boys and men were used to outdoor weather and conditions. It was late August and warm. Father was right, the clouds had rolled away and we knew our wet clothing would soon dry out.

As we walked along the top of the hill toward the berry patch, there were occasionally a few short blackberry bushes in the pastures or meadows loaded with small but exceptionally sweet berries. Father always stopped to pick these, telling me once that it was always a good idea to make sure of what we had now, for we never can be sure of what we may have or may not have in the future. I have often thought of that philosophy since, when I have seen people either picking berries or living their lives. There are always some who run from place to place leaving something fairly good behind them, always looking for something better ahead, and frequently finding that the pot at the end of the rainbow is only a will-o'-the-wisp.

After about an hour's walk, we arrived at the big slashing where the berries were. Around the turn of the century, there were more woods and more lumbering operations than there are now. After the trees in a piece of woods were lumbered off, if nothing further was done with the clearing, the first year a dense growth of weeds sprang up from the rank, highly fertile soil. In a year or two, the weeds were followed by raspberry bushes; then they gradually disappeared and the blackberry bushes came. Finally, they too died out, and were replaced by brush and small trees which in due course of years, if not disturbed, grew into a forest again. A year or so ago, I stood with a friend on a back lot on the farm where I lived most of my youth. Sixty years ago, I helped to plant potatoes on that lot. Today, it is covered with trees, some of which are a foot in diameter. Thus does nature restore itself to its original primeval status.

For the first few years after the trees were cut, these cleared places were known as slashings. Because the soil was new and rich, blackberry bushes in the slashings often grew higher than a man's head, and if the season had been right, the bushes would be almost black with big, luscious berries where one could fill a 2-quart pail almost without moving. Settlers used to tell stories about surprising bears in these slashings, with jaws dripping blood red with the juice of berries, which they had obtained by standing on their hind legs and using their front paws to swipe bushes of loaded berries into their mouths.

But there were no bears in the slashing when Father and I were there, although it was a rather formidable place. Underfoot were piles of rotten brush and pitfalls hard to see, because the bushes grew so high and close together. It took some courage and endurance to break a path through those bushes, for they were covered with thorns that made us look and feel as if we had done a battle with a wildcat. Most of the women berry pickers used to wear gloves which covered their entire hands with the exception of the fingertips. But men and boys scorned anything so sissified and feminine.

When we had broken our way into the slashing and gotten where the berries were, Father and I separated. I carefully located my big milk pail where I could be sure to find it, fastened my smaller pail to my belt, and I was ready for business.

Since then, when troubled by the stress of this complicated modern life, I have often wished that I had a retreat as remote and as peaceful as was that old-time berry patch. It was miles distant from the nearest human habitation. Nearby, a catbird (the northern mocking bird), disturbed by my presence, kept calling me a thief. Beyond the slashing, in the distant hill pasture, I could hear the lonesome tinkle, tinkle, tinkle of a little bell on the collar of a buck sheep leading his flock. At first I heard Father crashing through the brush and bushes. Then, even that sound was gone, and I was more alone than I have ever been in my life since—a good feeling and a good place to search your own soul.

To be sure, there were mosquitoes and flies in there and it was hot! But I soon learned that if I was going to get any berries picked, I had to stop spending my time slapping mosquitoes. That bit of philosophy of not letting small annoyances interfere with our goals is one which I have since often found useful.

While working quietly to fill my pails, almost afraid to break the quiet even by whistling, a stick cracked under my foot and I almost jumped out of my skin when the deep silence was broken by a crash and whir-r-r of wings as a partridge flew up, almost between my legs, and sailed away over the bushes. I still remember the chills that went up and down my back. Coming from almost under my feet, I wondered if the bird had a nest there. Carefully parting the bushes, I found it. The nest—close to an old log—was built of old leaves, a few feathers, grass, and roots. I counted eleven whitish eggs, smaller than hen's eggs. They were speckled with spots of brown. I backed away, hoping that I had not disturbed them so that she would not come back.

\* \* \*

Mother used to tell a blood-curdling and true story of what happened to her and her sister Hattie when they went after blackberries down in the big slashing in the woods that bordered their farm. It was Civil War times and Mother's father and older brother were away at war. Food was scarce and her mother made sure that they picked and canned all the different kinds of berries they could find.

On this particular day, the two girls had gotten their pails full and were about ready to start for home when they heard a terrifying roar. It was a blood-curdling sound—different from anything they had ever heard.

Grabbing their pails, they started for home as fast as they could go through the path to the woods that led out into the open pasture. Every few minutes they heard that awful roar, and each time it sounded a little closer. Finally, the girls were so frightened that they put the pails of berries down so they could run faster.

After what seemed an eternity of time, they came to the open pasture and stopped to look up along the hill where the woods met the pasture. Sure enough, there was a strange-looking animal there, bigger than any dog they had ever seen. They knew that it was no dog. As they looked, the animal roared again. Then the girls ran for their lives, never stopping until they reached their home.

After they had caught their breath, the girls told their mother about the strange animal. She laughed it off but all the same she was impressed, for badly as she needed those berries, she didn't make the girls go back to get them.

Later that day, two men came to the house and asked if any of the family had seen a big animal. My grandmother told them what the children had just seen. The man said there had been a circus at Danby village, a lion had gotten loose and they had not found it yet. In telling the story, Mother said that a whole gang of men hunted the lion all day, and she added,

Home from the blackberry patch or slashing. Besides being fun to pick, blackberries Day Before Yesterday added much to the family larder and their sale often helped the family finances.

with a twinkle in her eye, that she was sure that some of the neighborhood boys and men who were searching were fervently hoping that *they* would not be the ones to find the lion. Finally, toward night, the circus men found the lion in some weeds not far from

45

Mother's home. They said the lion was lonesome and hungry and had had enough of freedom. Then they sent word that they had captured the lion and there was no need to be afraid any longer. The next day, my grandmother sent the girls back after the berries, but she made an older brother go with them.

\* \* \*

When I got my big pail full, both the sun and my stomach told me that it was getting near noon, so I made my way slowly and with some difficulty out of the bushes and found Father with his pail full, waiting for me by a spring where the water was gushing out in such profusion that it formed a little brook running down the hill. I'll never forget how good that clear, cool water tasted when I threw myself flat and drank my fill of it.

\* \* \*

To rest after quenching my thirst, I lay down for a few minutes by the big rock that overshadowed the spring. Suddenly, in low tones, Father said, "Don't move, Eddie—don't move!"

I lay still except that I rolled my eyes trying to see what had startled Father. I saw all right! Not three feet from me, lying next to the rock, was a big snake. And on the other side of me was another! Each of the snakes was about three feet long, one a little longer than the other. At that moment, they seemed bigger than crocodiles. The one nearest me was making a dry, raspy noise. I shut my eyes and stopped looking.

After the longest moment I have ever spent, Father spoke again, "It's all right, Eddie. Thank God, they've gone!"

Then he told me that they were banded or timber rattlesnakes, poisonous and dangerous. Then he went on to tell me that the pioneers found many rattlesnakes in southern and western New York, but that he had been surprised to see them now as they seldom got so far north.

\* \* \*

You can bet that I was a tired, hungry, but happy boy when Father and I got those berries home and proudly showed them to Mother.

But that was not the end of the story. Those were hard times during the nineties and the family was short of money. So, after dinner, Father hitched a horse to the old buggy. We loaded in the berries and I drove to the distant villages to sell them. After hitching the horse in the church sheds, I took a pail of the berries and started peddling them around the village. Almost every housewife bought some. Most of the women were scrupulously fair in measuring out an exact quart from my big pail. But there were some, however, who filled the measuring cup as high as they could without the berries rolling off. Then they would jar the cup to settle the berries so they could put on a few more. So my berries never measured up to as many as I thought I had.

What did I get for them? Just five cents a quart, or about $1.50 for both Father's and my day's work. But it was fun and I would like to find one of those old slashings again. Better still, how I would like a big piece of pie made with those big luscious wild blackberries, just like Mother used to make. How about you?

*Postscript:*

A few days after this book was written, a friend and I did find a blackberry slashing. There had been a bad drought so the berries were few and small, but the bushes were just as high and mean as ever. We got a pint of berries and enough scratches and strained muscles breaking through the bushes and brush to cure me of blackberry slashings for the rest of my life.

Thus do the fond memories of youth fade with the stern realities of age!

## CHAPTER SIX

# HORSE LAUGHS

**W**HEN WE MOVED TO OUR FARM IN 1943, THERE WERE horses on every farm in the neighborhood. When we left that farm in 1957, just 14 years later, there was not a single working horse left. That's how fast progress—or at least change—has come. A middle-aged farmer said to me just recently, with a nostalgic gleam in his eye, "Ed, I miss my horses. You can damn a tractor but you can't love one! Farmers lost something when the horses went." Then he and I got to visiting about some of the adventures and misadventures that we had with horses when we were young.

I started by telling him about a farmer for whom I worked, who kept several vicious horses. One of them would kick the daylights out of you if you didn't watch her every minute. I used to clean her off with a currycomb with a long handle so that I could reach her from the next stall. Maybe I was fascinated also by making her try to knock off the boards of the stable back of her.

This same farmer had a team which I drove to take the milk to the factory. One morning I delivered the milk to the butter factory all right and got the cans full of skim milk to bring back to the farm to feed the calves and pigs. In order to get some groceries, I hitched the horses in the church shed near the butter factory while I went across the road to the store. I came back to the wagon with my arms full of groceries, put them in around the milk cans, and started to go up by the team to unhitch them. I never got there. Before I could untie them, they rammed backwards out of the shed with great violence, breaking the reins with which they were tied, cramped the wheels sideways, and turned the wagon over. The skim milk spilled out of the cans, making an awful mess of the groceries. One of the horses got tangled in the harness and fell down. To stop his thrashing around, I ran and sat on his head. Mr. Blanchard, the storekeeper across the road, saw all the fracas, came running across the street, and with his help we finally got the horse on his feet, the wagon righted, and the cans—now empty—back into the wagon.

I started sadly for home, all the time wondering what my boss and his wife were going to say but defending myself with the thought that the old son-of-a-gun hadn't told me that the team was what we used to call "pullers," horses that never would wait to be untied. Facing the farmer with all the courage I could muster, I told him what happened. I never will forget what the kindly old fellow said, "Don't let it worry you, boy. *That* team will do it sometimes. Should have told you."

There was another neighbor for whom I worked during the next summer. Every morning I got up at half past four, walked a mile or so to this neighbor's farm, helped him with the chores, and ate breakfast. Then I harnessed Molly to a stone boat, loaded on a one-horse cultivator, and climbed a steep dug road up a mountain to a big field of corn and potatoes on the plateau at the top. I held that cultivator while Molly hauled it back and forth, back and forth, through that corn and potato field during the long summer days. At noon, I fed Molly her oats and ate my lunch, rested a few moments, and started all over again. One can't work in close companionship with a faithful horse like that without growing to love her.

At five o'clock, we went back down off the mountain. I fed and took care of the horse, helped with the milking, and walked home. That's the way I spent my summer vacation. Incidentally, it was good for me. I wish every boy in America today could have the same experience. There just wasn't any time to raise the devil. But this is a story about horses.

While I was working for that same man, he sent me to market one day with a load of eggs in an enclosed cart, much like the modern milk cart except it was drawn by horses. The cart was hauled by a staid old horse and a colt that had not been hitched up more than two or three times. While crossing a bridge, we stirred up a bees' nest and they immediately began stinging the horses. The old horse could take it but the young one couldn't, so she began to run while the other one held back at first. I had little control over the team because the lines passed through narrow slits in the front of the enclosed cart. So I jumped out of the open door at the side of the cart and raced to catch the colt by the head. I almost made it but not

quite. In despair, I watched that team run away with the cartfull of eggs, swaying crazily from one side of the road to the other. Now haven't you at some time in your life, after you have had something terrible happen to you, said to yourself, "Oh, I was so happy just a few moments ago and didn't know enough to know it. Now, look at me."

Well, that's the way I felt.

The team finally ran themselves out down the valley road, ending up of their own accord with their heads against the side of a barn. We finally got the eggs to market, and glory of glories, there were only about half a dozen broken. The only thing the kindly owner, my boss, said was, "My fault, Eddie, I should never have asked you to drive that colt." Then he winked at me and walked away.

Another horse friend of mine with whom I worked for most of one summer was Old Dave. I liked him, but he surely had ideas of his own. And when he got one of those ideas in his head, he took over. This particular summer, Dave and I cultivated corn and potatoes on a steep side hill. It was the custom of the lady of the house to ring a big farm bell on the porch when it was dinner time. Dave got so busy along about noon, trying to listen for that bell, that he would stagger all over the corn instead of walking between the rows as he should. When driving a horse to cultivate, I always had the lines tied together around my back so as to leave my hands free to guide the cultivator. One day at noon, the bell rang, and in spite of everything I could do, Dave turned at right angles to the rows—and horse, cultivator, and boy went sailing down through the corn and potatoes, plowing them out! Dave never stopped until he landed on the horse barn floor all ready for his oats. One could see that blank place in those crops all the rest of the summer, and every time my boss noticed it, he got mad all over again and gave me the devil.

No village Day Before Yesterday was quite complete without a horse dealer or trader. With some of them you had to watch your step or you might lose your shirt.

Even so, there were horse deals that were satisfactory to all concerned. This story concerns a farmer by the name of Harris and a horse dealer by the name of Thompson. The farmer tried to buy a horse from the dealer, but all he was willing to pay was $100 and the dealer wanted $300. So the dealer wouldn't sell and the deal fell through. Some time later, Thompson found his horse dead. Accordingly, he telephoned the farmer saying that he had changed his mind and was now willing to sell the horse for $100 providing he got a check in advance. The dealer got the check and delivered the dead horse in the night on the farmer's lawn. Strange to say, there was no protest from the farmer. Finally, the dealer happened to meet him one day on the street. He couldn't stand the suspense any longer, so he asked,

"Did you receive the horse, Mr. Harris?"

"Oh, yes," said Harris.

"Well, didn't you find him dead?"

"Yes."

"Well, what did you do with him?"

"Sold him for $500."

"$500," yelled the dealer. "How did you do that?"

"I raffled him off for $5 a bid to 100 bidders."

"Yeah, well how about the feller who got the lucky number. Was he mad? Didn't he raise hell when he found he had won a dead horse?"

"No, he was all right. I gave him his $5 back."

Perhaps the best horse trading story is the one, also said to be true, that Abraham Lincoln used to tell on himself. He and his friend, the judge, agreed to trade horses, sight unseen. Agreeing to meet at a certain time with their horses in the public square, Lincoln returned with a carpenter's sawhorse over his shoulder. After some delay, the judge, who had scoured the whole locality, came back with a horse that could hardly stand up—what with all the diseases with which it was very apparently afflicted. Lincoln took one look at the animal, handed him the sawhorse, and said, "You win!"

Not far from the milk station where we delivered our milk, there was a corner where several roads converged. This mean farmer, whom we will call Jake, had at least one good characteristic. He kept good horses, and he took care of them. One was a road horse —a roan who really could travel when he had to. Occasionally, there might be three or four dairymen coming down the roads that led to the corner. Whenever Old Jake was one of them, he would set his horse at a fast trot and beat the others to the milk station.

A young friend of mine, whom we will call Bob, often delivered the milk from his farm. In common with several other farmers, he got exceedingly tired of Old Jake's discourtesy and selfishness. So Bob managed to use the best horse on his father's farm every day for a while with which to deliver the milk, believing that his horse was just as fast—if not faster— than Old Jake's. Bob had to wait for a few days so as to time his approach to the corner about the same time as Jake's.

One morning when the occasion was just right, Jake saw two or three milk wagons approaching the corner from different directions. As usual, he started up his horse to beat them out. Among those two or three was Bob, who also put his horse into a fast trot. He went around the wagon ahead of him and reached the corner at almost exactly the same time that Jake did. Then both of them urged their horses into a gallop and raced like mad to get to the milk station first. Jake was just a little ahead, but, determined to the point of recklessness, Bob pulled out around him. To avoid being sideswiped, Jake yanked his horse to one side, the wheels of his wagon went into the ditch, the wagon lurched once or twice and then went over, spilling milk all over the landscape. Fortunately, it hurt nothing but Jake's feeilngs, so no one wasted any sympathy on him. Moreover, he was cured, for after that he made no further effort to get

52

into the line at the milk station before his turn.

One autumn in the horse-and-buggy days when I was vice-principal of a high school, Mr. Barford, the principal and I secured the loan of a horse for the winter from my brother who lived on a farm over the mountain.

When Fay loaned us the horse, he told us that we could have all the apples we wanted if we would pick them ourselves. So Mr. Barford and I hitched Nellie to the democrat wagon and went over the hill to get the apples. We worked until it was almost dark, loaded the wagon full of apples, and started over the hill for home.

About halfway up the mountain road, Nellie decided that she wouldn't pull the load any farther. In other words, she balked. Nothing that we could do or say—and we said plenty—could induce Nellie to take another step. What to do? It was dark and cold. Finally, we had to unload *all* the apples and leave them beside the road. Then, and not until then, would Nellie consent to move. And not, mind you, with us *in* the wagon. Every time we got in, the horse balked. So we walked all the way home.

When I told Fay about his darned old balky horse, he just laughed and said, "Nellie was smarter than you were."

The only good thing about the incident was that we didn't have an audience when Nellie balked, for to have a horse balk was always highly embarrassing and a very hilarious event to everyone who saw it, except the driver. The "roadside superintendents" were always willing to offer plenty of advice on how to start a balky horse, such as putting a burr under his tail or tickling his belly. Such remedies, like most free advice, were no good, since a balker is usually a kicker also. Instead of starting with any of the inducements offered, the horse would often kick the wagon to pieces back of him and the slats out of you if you got too near to his business end.

One driver took the advice of an onlooker and built a small fire under the balky horse. It worked! The horse started up just far enough to leave the fire exactly under the wagon back of him. Then there was a mad scramble to unhitch the wagon and back it away before it burned up.

In the early days of rural free delivery (R.F.D.), I knew a mailman who had a balky horse. The mailman was very heavy, and often when the horse got

When the horses bent into their collars together and the plow turned the furrow just right, it was pleasant to smell the newly turned earth, to feel the springtime sun on your back, and to do a good day's work.

tired of hauling him, he would stop and refuse to go on until the driver got out and walked ahead of him down the road. Then, after a while, the mailman would ride again until the horse took it in his head to balk. When asked about it, the mailman would never admit that his horse balked. No owner ever would. He just said, "I don't know any better way to reduce my weight than to walk. Do you?" Putting it that way, you had to agree with him.

There is a sad ending to that story. The mailman had a long-standing heart ailment. One day his balky horse made him walk too much and he had a fatal heart attack.

Prince, a horse I owned more recently, was a lovable old cuss that surely had his ideas about things. One of them was the nice habit of deliberately lying down when a job seemed a little difficult for him. One day, I was plowing a drainage ditch on a steep pitch just a short distance above a main traveled highway. In the process, the drainage plow didn't pull as easily as Prince thought it should, so he carefully laid down on the downhill side. I had to take off every strap of his harness before he would condescend to get up again. What made me swearing mad was that it seemed to me that every friend I had in the world took *that* particular time to go up or down the highway, slow up, and shout some insult at me.

But the horse I loved most was Molly, the one I owned and kept on the farm long after I had tractors and after I had any real need for her. Molly had plenty of spirit, was very intelligent, and I think she was the gentlest creature I have ever known. Children or adults could climb all over her and she would always act as if she liked it. But Molly had one peculiarity. It wasn't safe to leave her alone, unhitched. She would never break anything or injure herself, but if she thought no one was looking, she would turn quietly around and go back to her stable every time.

Finally, there came a sad morning when we went out to the barn and found that Molly's gentle spirit had fled. We felt as if we had lost a member of the family.

The other day at lunch, Dr. Earl E. Clarke, Dean of Students at Ithaca College, got to talking with me about some of his adventures in growing up in the horse-and-buggy days on a prairie ranch in North Dakota.

Even more than it ever was here in the East, all the Great West was a land of horses. No one moved anywhere without horses, either in the saddle or behind a team.

Earl's father always kept a herd of horses. When not in use, they were allowed to run more or less wild, coming in to the home buildings only when they needed a drink of water.

One afternoon when Earl was about 12 years old, his father said:

"The horses haven't been in to drink for some time. You take your brother (about 10 years old) and go round them up and bring them back."

So with both Earl and his brother mounted on a single pony, they started out. Every time they came to a ranch house (and those houses were miles apart), they stopped to inquire if their horses had been seen. Each time the answer was "yes." So after stopping several times to inquire, they finally found the horses many miles from home.

By this time it was growing dark and beginning to snow. The wind was howling and it was very cold. The boys rounded up the horses and started them for home. The only guide they had was the natural instinct of the horses to go home, but since the horses were half wild, this was not a very reliable guide.

After a while, the younger boy claimed that they were going in the wrong direction and that they should turn around, but Earl insisted that their only hope was to trust the herd. By now it was hard even to do this, because the blizzard was raging so that the horses were but dim shadows ahead of them.

In telling the story, Earl said that he was never so scared in his life. He knew what sometimes happened to people caught out in North Dakota blizzards.

"The most wonderful thing I have ever seen in my life," said Earl, "was a dim light in the window of a neighbor's ranch house."

From there on, they found their way and soon were home, where they got a welcome from their worried parents who had almost given them up for lost.

I might add that those young boys brought up to habits of work and responsibility *brought home the horses*—and Earl has been bringing them home ever since!

Some credit should also be given the boys' pony who carried both of them, plodding on mile after mile, and finally getting them safely home.

On that same ranch, Earl's father raised thousands of Herefords for beef. Now I have grown Herefords, and the cows in a small herd are the gentlest of creatures. But every rancher and cowboy in the West knows that Herefords and all the other breeds are dangerous to a man on foot, because the men who work them are always on horseback, and, in more recent years, in cars.

One day when Earl was young, he rode out to inspect a great herd of Herefords with his father and a cattle buyer in the first automobile ever in that section. A cow of any breed has more curiosity than any other animal I have ever known. Within minutes after they arrived in the car near the cattle, they were completely surrounded by the white-faced Herefords coming from all directions until more than 200 of the animals had converged around the car, as close as they could get—and no doubt wondering about the new contraption and the two-legged animals in it. Earl said that that great sea of white faces looking at him was a strange and never-to-be-forgotten experience.

Another one of Dr. Clarke's stories was about the experience he had when he was awakened in the night by his mother, who told him that his younger brother was very ill and that he must get on his pony and ride fast to get the doctor. The physician lived six miles away and it was very cold.

If you remember how hard it was for you when you were 12 years old to have to get up in the night to do an errand or to start the farm chores at four or five o'clock in the morning, you will know how Earl felt.

In addition to it being a cold and lonely ride, he was scared for fear his brother would die before he could bring the doctor back. But he made the journey all right, roused the doctor from his sleep, and helped him to hitch up his horse. Then pulling the big buffalo robe about their legs, the doctor and Earl set out with the horse and cutter, with Earl's pony following.

Arriving at daylight, they found that Earl's mother had taken matters into her own hands—as women of her generation had a habit of doing—and had kept the boy submerged up to his chin in very warm water, a standard home cure for the croup. The doctor examined the boy carefully for symptoms of pneumonia. Finding none, he commended the mother for doing just the right thing. Then he ate a hearty breakfast with the family and set out for another day of calls on sick patients. And, like so many other country doctors of his time, he didn't know when he would have any opportunity to catch up on his lost sleep.

\* \* \*

When Tenney, my Texas-reared daughter-in-law, was a 15-year-old girl, there was a heavy rainstorm, almost a cloudburst, in western Texas where she lived. The rain flooded the lowlands along the river bottom and a draw where Mr. Williams, Tenney's father, pastured a flock of 200 sheep. Tenney tells the story of how she and her father rescued the sheep with the help of the horses.

"Dad and I drove our flock onto a shush pit dam or knoll to temporary safety. Then we were forced to run and get a wagon and load the sheep into it, 25 at a time, in order to carry them to safety.

There was a satisfaction driving a team like this never to be had from a modern tractor.

58

"It went pretty well at first but the water was coming up fast and furiously, until finally, with the last load, the water was swirling around us so high that the horses were unable to pull the wagon out loaded with sheep.

"Believe me, I was scared, but Dad knew what to do. We were on horses, so, crowding his horse alongside the team, Dad reached down with a knife and cut the horses loose from the wagon. They lost no time in getting out of the flood and rushed for home. Then with our horses, we carried the 25 sheep, one at a time, from the wagon to safety.

"Unfortunately, by the time we had rescued the last of the sheep, I got caught on the wrong side of the now furiously raging stream, so that I could not get home that night without traveling many miles up around the head of the draw. Our only neighbor on that side was a shiftless sort of a fellow who lived in a small, dilapidated shack with a large family, but he was kind enough to invite me to stay all night. Wet and cold, I had no alternative, so I accepted. I never will forget that sleepless night. The bed which I shared with two little girls had many other very active occupants—bedbugs! To add insult to all my other grievances, when I finally got home the next day, Mother made me take off all my clothes before she would let me into the house!"

* * *

Not long ago, I drove down through the hamlet where we lived and where I worked on neighboring farms. No longer there were the country grocery and the milk factory to which I had delivered the milk.

Long since gone was the kind country storekeeper who had helped me to untangle my team; and gone too, of course, was kindly Old John who collected bad horses, but who was as good a boss as a boy could ever have just the same. Fallen in ruins also were the church sheds, one of the last reminders of the horse-and-buggy days.

Yes, I loved horses. They got me into scrapes sometimes, but most of them were as good friends and companions as a boy or man could have.

## CHAPTER SEVEN

# THEY GOT THERE JUST THE SAME

ONE TIME DAY BEFORE YESTERDAY MY FATHER, Fay, an older brother, and I were loading hay on a steep side hill onto a lumber wagon with a big hay rigging. Father and Fay were pitching the hay up to me on the load. When we had the load almost on, the high rear wheel of the old wagon on the lower hillside suddenly crumbled to pieces, letting the wagon down, so that the hay slid off downhill, taking me with it. When I finally dug myself out, I sat down with the others to contemplate the ruin. I never saw my father nearer tears than he was then. Without the wagon, he was out of business, and it was as difficult for him then to buy a new wagon as it would be for a poor farmer today to buy a new tractor. But what had to be, had to be. So the next day, Fay came home from town proudly driving a shiny, brand-new lumber wagon. When he arrived with the new wagon, we took off the big box, put on the hay rigging and finished the haying.

The lumber wagon was an all-round farm tool. I do not know why it was so named, unless it was because it was sometimes used to transport logs and lumber. Equipped with a hay rigging, it was used to harvest all the grain and hay. With its big box with extra boards on top, the lumber wagon became the vehicle in which cash crops like potatoes were moved to the railroad. I can still close my eyes and hear the distant rumble of a lumber wagon, with a farmer returning from market on a late fall evening on some nearby back road.

When I ride in a warm closed car today, I often think of those old-time vehicles and their riders, who had little or no protection from the elements. Time and again, the drivers got wet through or very cold, but they were used to it and I don't think they had more colds than we do now.

While the wagon was still new and shiny, Fay and I went to market with it and he condescended to let me drive for a little way. To me, that was just as wonderful as driving a car for the first time would be to a modern boy. While Fay was standing in the wagon box back of the seat, I turned around to say something to him and the horses took that moment to drag the new wagon right through the only big mudhole in the road for miles, splashing the new paint on the wagon from one end to the other. Grabbing the reins away from me, Fay snarled, "You dumb cluck! Always yak-yakking, never paying attention to your business!"

You know how brothers are!

* * *

Not long ago, I read a Berkshire, New York, news item republished from the August 22, 1891 issue of the local country weekly. It read:

"Two more surreys in town, making seven in all. This time, the fortunate owners are Charles Manning and Dr. R. D. Eastman."

The item, written 70 years ago, is of more than ordinary interest to me because I was born in Berkshire, and Dr. Eastman, my uncle, helped me into this uncertain and precarious world. It is also interesting because it shows how completely our world of transportation has changed in one lifetime.

Old-timers will remember the surreys and, as the news item indicated, will remember how the ownership of a surrey put you in the "top ten" in any old-time village or neighborhood. The surrey was a bright and shiny vehicle, with two seats that had some kind of upholstery, and over all was a top, gaily festooned with a fringe of tassels running all the way around the edge. Of course, the outfit was not complete unless it was driven by a team of well-matched road horses with a light harness kept well oiled and shiny.

With horses, my uncle could compete with any of them. Because he was a country doctor constantly on the go, almost day and night, he took pride in having a stable full of the best horses he could buy. But the surrey was only for the very special occasions when Uncle or other owners wanted to ride out in style, and, being human, wanted to show off a little.

Generally, however, Uncle had little time for such nonsense. He drove the hills and valleys of northern Tioga County for I don't know how many thousands

of miles during 50 years of practice with a horse and buggy.

The buggy was the chief mode of transportation when there was little baggage to be carried. Next to the surrey, a buggy with hard rubber tires was the last word in "high falutin" style. Remember those hard rubber tires? If you do, you're dated! They came long before inflated tires of course, but the hard rubber made the buggy ride a little easier. In many cases, the rubber tires on a shiny buggy hitched to a lively horse surely enabled a young fellow to have his choice of the pretty girls in the neighborhood.

Human nature being what it is and never changing, the chief difference between the boys and girls of Day Before Yesterday and those of today is in their mode of transportation. The young fellow and his girl with a horse and buggy couldn't travel as far as a couple with a modern car, but on the other hand, they didn't have to. The roads were not so crowded and there were many secluded spots. It is nice to think of the romances and the lifelong marriages that had their beginning in the old-time buggies, with the horse standing half asleep and the reins over the dashboard, so that Grandpa, when he was a boy, could give full attention to Grandma when she was a girl.

An interesting feature of the buggy was the narrow step between the high wheels that a rider had to reach for with his foot in order to get into the vehicle. The brief glimpse of the lady's ankle, displayed when she stepped into the high buggy, fully repaid the hired man for hitching up the horse for her. Those were the days, you will remember, when a lady's ankle was a rare and intriguing sight, since the skirts practically dragged on the ground. In these days of short-shorts and bikinis, the old-time hired man must be wondering what the world has come to.

Another very useful vehicle of the horse-and-buggy days was the democrat wagon. I am not certain why it was so named, but I am sure that it had no connection with politics, for otherwise, in those bitter partisan days, no good Republican would be caught dead in a democrat wagon. Maybe the vehicle got its name because it was big enough to put in two or three seats and load in the whole family—Pa, Ma, and nine kids, the hired man—and yes, even Rover. Come to think of it, Rover wasn't like these modern coddled pets of today. He usually traveled on his own power, alongside the wagon, roaming the fields on either side so that he actually traveled twice as far as the wagon did.

How many of you remember the gig and the dog-cart? They were two-wheel vehicles of the old days, each drawn by one horse, the chief difference being in the elegance of the gig, which, like the surrey, often sported a gay top or canopy. The dog-cart was a plain, everyday citizen without springs, which you fully realized when it jerked you along with every movement of the horse. The only reminder of the old two-wheel gig and the dog-cart is the modern rubber-tired racing gig or cart. How I used to marvel, when I was a kid, at the great courage of those drivers who put on dark glasses, braced their heels in holders in the thills, and drove their racehorses at breakneck speed around the racetrack at fair time.

* * *

How did the old-timers get around in the wintertime Day Before Yesterday? In the first place, it is necessary to remember that sleighing in the northern states usually started early in the winter, even as

63

early as Thanksgiving time, and lasted until spring. The snow was not shoveled off the roads or worn off by cars and trucks as it is today. As soon as the first snow came, it was packed down by the traffic and every snowfall improved the sleighing.

Since the snow was not cleaned off the roads, it was often necessary to take to the fields. I've driven right over the top of fences buried deep in the drifts. Sometimes it was necessary for all the men of the neighborhood to come out with teams and shovels to break out the roads. Sometimes people were snowbound for several days, which could mean serious trouble in case of sickness or some other emergency.

If a young fellow wanted to take a girl out in style, he was lucky to have (or to be able to borrow from his dad) a swell-body cutter, drawn by a high-stepping, good-looking horse. Now it was really fun to be together in one of those cutters, with a warm robe wrapped tightly around you and your girl, and a warm soapstone at your feet.

There was just one drawback. Those cutters tipped over easily, especially when the snow had drifted so that one side of the track was higher than the other. It was hard, also, not to tip the cutter over when you

Democrat wagon was a utility vehicle that may be likened to the modern station wagon.

were trying to turn it around. However, tumbling out of the upset cutter with your girl into the soft snow was not always a misfortune if you could keep the horse from running away, and especially if your girl fell into your arms. Maybe it gave you the chance to get your arm around her, which you wouldn't dare to do when you were riding without mishap.

64

A ride in a swell body cutter with a warm robe over your lap and a soapstone at your feet was one of the nicest things about winter.

The late Dean Carl E. Ladd of Cornell University used to tell a story about going to a wedding in a cutter with his mother.

"I put the cuff buttons through one end of my double starched cuffs," said Carl, "and fastened each to the wrist part of my shirt with a hidden cuff holder or clip. The cuffs were reversible. When the front end got dirty, I turned them around so that only the clean end showed.

"I hitched up Old Tom, put some straw in the bottom of the cutter and put a fur blanket under the robe, for it was a very cold day. Mother brought out a soapstone all wrapped up in a woolen cloth and we started out. Although I had mittens, I had to sit on my hands once in a while to keep them warm.

"Old Tom trotted along, blowing steam out of his nostrils. The steam drifted back, covering his shoulders and sides with a white frost. All went well until we started down the long Townley's hill. One side of the cutter struck a drift and over we went with Mother, the soapstone, the seat cushions, and me—spread all over the roadside.

"Immediately, Tom ran away, but I hung onto the reins. I was flat on my belly with my overcoat riding through the snow like a bobsled. I lifted my chin and rode with my arms stretched out in front, hanging onto the reins while the snow pushed up into my coat sleeves until it was packed to the elbows. Finally, we reached the end of the hill. Tom got tired of dragging me and stopped. We went back, loaded Mother and the things back into the cutter, and went

Sleighing came early and went late Day Before Yesterday.

on to attend the wedding ceremony. Just before it took place, Mother caught hold of me, tied my necktie, tried to paste back one lock of hair, and pulled down my coat a little. I guess she thought I was a bedraggled son, but I could see that she was rather satisfied because I didn't let Old Tom get away. But I wasn't able to forget those wet, cold, ruined cuffs until I was able to fill up on the wedding dinner, including about 16 kinds of frosted cakes.''

\* \* \*

Every farmer, Day Before Yesterday, had a long-sleigh which corresponded in usefulness to the democrat wagon. The box of the longsleigh was set on long runners in which it was possible to put in either two seats or just one, leaving the back part of the sleigh in which to take light produce to market and bring home groceries and feed for the cattle.

But the bobsleighs were the farmers' most useful winter vehicles. They were two separate units or sleighs hitched together with a "reach." On these, a farmer could put a long box and transport almost anything, or a hay rigging on which he could move loose hay and grain in the wintertime. With the box or rigging off, the farmer could roll logs onto the bobsleighs from the skidways in the woods and move the logs to the mill for lumber or to the house for firewood.

One of my older brothers—then a bachelor who had taken considerable kidding because he seemed to be shy of all females—started with his bobsleighs up the long hill road after a load of logs. After a short distance, he overtook Angelina, a maiden lady of no uncertain years but whose reputation in the neighborhood was somewhat "blowed" upon. We happened to be watching from our house and saw the lady stop my brother, apparently thumbing a ride. Out of the kindness of his heart, he permitted her to climb onto the rear bobsled, where her perch was rather precarious. The last we saw of them as they disappeared up the hill, Brother was sitting erect and stiff, and, I am sure, highly embarrassed, driving his team from the front bobsled while Angelina rode like a queen on the back one. We never permitted Brother to forget that adventure!

Another very nice thing about bobsleighs was that, with the big box on, they could be—and frequently were—used for straw rides. Ever go on one? Plenty of clean straw was loaded into the bottom of the big long box and the young people got into the straw with warm blankets over their laps. Then with a lively team and a string of jingling musical sleigh bells on each horse, they were off for a long ride through the clear, cold, starlit night with the snow crackling under the runners of the sleds. As they rode, they laughed and sang the popular ballads of the day and were happy and carefree.

Somewhere in the middle of the ride, the party would end up at a friend's house, where there would be hot cocoa, lots to eat, and plenty of appetite to go with the food. This was followed perhaps by games or dancing, and then again into the sleighs for the ride home—this time, maybe sleepy and tired but still happy. Nothing would be heard except perhaps some quiet conversation and the jingling of the sleigh bells.

\* \* \*

Often, as I ride in a modern car, covering in an hour what used to take us a day, I think of the slow, easy pace of the horse-and-buggy days, and I sometimes wonder if we didn't get just as far in real achievement and happiness.

# CHAPTER EIGHT

# "THEM HORSELESS WAGONS"

REMEMBER THE FIRST CAR YOU EVER HAD? I'LL BET you do, for if you are like me, you had more fun with it than any car you have had since.

Recently, I had a mild case of "car-itis." I looked at a lot of small, foreign cars, as well as at some of our standard American ones. Then I got over my "car-itis" by settling for fixing up my old one. The experience got me to thinking of the fun and the adventures my friends and I have had with automobiles.

The first car I ever saw came near to being the last one. I was a boy driving old Prince hitched to a buggy. Coming toward us, roaring and snorting at the unheard of speed of maybe 12 or 15 miles per hour, was one of those strange monsters that I had read about but had never seen. I was scared! So was old Prince. In spite of hell and high water, and in spite of all my efforts to keep him in the road, the horse turned squarely around, just missed turning the buggy over, and went away from there fast. After my father and older brother had one or two similar experiences, we never dared take old Prince on the road again, and the neighbors all agreed that there "ought to be a law agin' allowin' those new-fangled horseless wagons on the road." Sometimes since, I have wondered if they were not right.

I'll bet that you well remember the first time you ever rode in a car. I do. I had just been married. There was only one car in the village, and, by golly, our friends hadn't owned it long before they asked us to go for a ride. The women wore big floppy hats, fastened by veils that tied under their chins. The men wore long nightgown affairs they called dusters. Remember them? Then we went sailing down the valley at the terrific speed of 15 miles per hour, kind of scared, but it was an adventure we never forgot.

Time rolled along, as it has a habit of doing, until we bought *our* first car. I loved the darn thing but

I was afraid of it. I can still remember the nice new smell of gasoline and paint whenever I opened the barn door. (Yes, I said barn door. There were few garages then.) Shortly after we bought it, we invited a friend to go for a ride. A mile or two out of the village, I detected a little squeak or rumble, thought the thing was going to fall apart, so I turned around and drove it home just as fast as I could get there. I soon learned that rattles are a part of the nature of the beast.

You "old-timers" will remember about tires. We seldom made a trip of any length without having to climb out, often in the rain, and with suitable language pry a flat off, get the tube out and patch it, and then with a lot of energy and more language, get the tire on and inflated again. You will recall too, when you were in the middle of such an operation, how some "friend" would go sailing by and yell at you, "Get a horse!" One time when that happened to me, I caught up with the friend down the road a piece fixing his own tire, and I had the pleasure of returning the compliment, "Get a horse yourself!"

A friend of mine, middle-aged before he began driving a car, started to put his car in the barn one day. Once inside the barn, he forgot how to stop the car and went right through the side of the barn into the yard outside, yelling all the time so you could hear him three miles, "Whoa, Whoa! Damn ya, Whoa!"

I was riding with that same friend when we came to a steep pitch on the dirt road that had a good sprinkling of stones. Leaning forward stiff on the seat, and clutching the wheel with a "do or die" look on his face, Fred guided the car unsteadily down the hill. Bringing the car to a full stop, he turned, shook his fists at the rocks behind us and said to me, "There! I'll give you five dollars for every damn rock I missed!"

I was telling a young friend of mine the other day that the first automobiles had whip sockets on the dashboard. My friend said, "What the deuce are whip sockets?" Times do change. In case you don't know what whip sockets were, they were placed on the corners of dashboards of buggies and other wagons to hold the whips needed to remind lazy horses that life was not all beer and skittles—or should I say oats and hay? It took some time for the car manufacturers to learn that cussing was more effec-

Those early owners were proud guys when the temperamental engine didn't balk or the tires leak.

tive than whips to make a balky, temperamental gasoline engine work.

Before the days of the sedan, in which—no matter what the weather is—you are as comfortable as you

71

are in your own home, what a scramble it was to get the top up and the side curtains buttoned onto the car before the storm hit you. Nothing will give you a better idea of how cars have changed than to think what it would be like to drive a couple of hundred miles today in an open car in the winter-time with no heater. And in those days of the open touring cars, with lots of room between the front and back seats, we made room for extras by putting camp stools in that space for some of the younger members of the party to sit on.

Along in the spring of the year when I got my first car, my family and I started from home to visit my mother, a trip of something less than 50 miles. I dreaded getting through the heavy traffic of the city of Ithaca, but I made it all right except that I had to stop at the top of State Street hill to let the engine stop boiling. But when I struck the dirt road beyond the city limits, my troubles really began.

I shall always wonder why the path masters ruined the country roads every spring by rounding the mud and the rocks into the middle of the road, making travel almost impossible until the weather had smoothed them out. That's the way it was that spring all the way to Mother's. To add to my troubles, it had been raining, so that the mud was two or three inches thick and mixed with sod and stones all the way. I drove in low gear most of the time. Remember how you had to operate the gear shifts with your feet?

I got along fairly well until I got out beyond Tobeytown, where the mud got deeper and deeper and the engine got hotter and hotter until it finally swore off and I "swore" on trying to crank the thing, expecting every minute that the crank would kick back and break my arm. But the thing just wouldn't start. Not even a woman is more temperamental than those first gasoline engines were.

It was dark. We were a long, long ways from home. Finally, while I kept struggling with the brute, I sent my little boy to a farmhouse to ask the farmer to bring a team and pull us out. He wouldn't do it, probably thinking that people who would clutter up the road with such things must suffer the consequences. Anyway, I kept cranking, sweating, and "talking" to the thing. I don't know which one of the three finally did it; maybe it was just the engine getting cooler, but finally it started and we arrived at Mother's in the night. I can drive that distance now in an hour.

When I became a county agricultural agent, I took that same car with me. In that whole big county, there were only a few miles of hard road. In terms of mechanical sturdiness, that car was just about the best one I ever owned, for I drove it many thousands of miles over mountainous roads in mud and snow, and it always brought me home. Well, almost always, for there was just one time it didn't.

One day I was due to speak in a distant part of the county. We had a friend visiting us, so I thought it would be nice for the family and this friend to come along, and while I was attending the meeting, they could climb to the tower at the top of a high mountain near where I was to speak.

Before the meeting, I took them as high up on the mountain as it was possible to drive. Then they started to walk the rest of the way. When I tried to turn the car around to go back to my meeting, it became stuck in the ditch and I got out to lift it and shove it onto the road. It came out much more easily than I expected and started right down that mountain road, with me right after it—lickety-split! I caught up with it before it had gained much momentum, but there was no time to open the little side door, so I leaped right over the top and finally got under the wheel. It was too late to stop it with the brakes on that steep road, so I pulled it into the bank. When I could get my breath, I got out to count the damage. The front axle was bent a little and that was all. My family and friend went on up the mountain, and I drove the car very carefully down the mountain to a blacksmith—there was no garage—who straightened the axle while I went to the meeting.

Late that afternoon, I went back up the mountain to where the family was waiting for me and started our drive back. But within a few miles of home, I suddenly felt a slight jar. The car then bumped along until I managed to stop it. Investigation showed that the blacksmith, in putting the wheel back on after fixing the axle, had forgotten to replace the nut, so that the wheel had stayed on all that distance, held in place only by the light hubcap.

The late H. E. Babcock, who was known as Ed to thousands of his friends, was one of the best-known and best-loved farm leaders the Northeast has ever had. He was an excellent automobile driver, but a fast one. One time when he was coming down a very steep city street, he happened to glance out of his

Spring Day in Ithaca
1906. But where is the
lady's veil and the gen-
tleman's duster? Note
that he is driving from
the horse and buggy
side.

window and saw a car wheel rolling along beside him—a little ahead. Ed said to a companion riding with him, "Somebody has lost a wheel." Then a second later, the car began to bump and he yelled, "My gosh! it's mine!"

At another time, Ed and I were going half way across the state to a cattle sale. Incidentally, Ed was the best judge of cattle I have ever known and was just about the best companion. Somewhere on this trip, the car began to bump violently. He stopped the car, jumped out and found that one of the rear tires had developed a big bump or bubble and was about to blow out. Ed didn't stop by the tire but ran around to the front of the car, hoping I would arrive by the

74

tire by the time something happened. Just as I got beside the tire, it blew with a bang! Ed always claimed that he could see blue sky under my feet as I went into the air. During the fracas, a big black dog standing nearby let out a yelp, and, with his tail between his legs, scuttled back to the house, whereupon an old woman came out on the run, yelling that we had shot her dog!

Long before young people can get a license to drive, almost all of them get "car-itis." My sons were no exception. I can't blame them, for frequently I have mild attacks myself. While they were still at home, one of the boys acquired an old car with no seat cushions, no floor boards, and no top. It had even lost its reputation. But by constant tinkering, the boys could keep it going.

Near where we lived at the time, there was a creek bordered by heavy brush and trees. The owner of the car enticed one of his brothers into it one day, and then, with the throttle wide open, they went down through that brush with the older brother hanging on for dear life and yelling at every bump. I'll never know how he did it, but the driver went on, over and through the brush and skipped the trees until he came to the high bank of the creek. Then they sailed over the edge and five or six feet down into the mud, sand, and water of the creek bed.

After fussing around for an hour or two, trying to get the old wreck out, they came to the house and asked me if I would help. Armed with picks and shovels, we returned to the scene of their crime and with prodigious labor in the mud and water, we dug the car loose. Then one of the boys got in to run the car out. He made the mistake of putting it in reverse gear and plunged the car back into the creek farther and deeper than ever! Enough was enough. I threw down my shovel and went home. Late in the evening, the boys drove in. They had prevailed on a kind-hearted neighbor to bring his team and pull the car out.

For years, while I worked in New York City, we lived on Long Island, and most of our relatives lived 225 miles upstate. So I have many vivid memories of driving an open car years ago, with children, including a small baby, all the way upstate from New York City. Often we would have to stop and ask some housewife if we could warm the milk for the baby, over her stove.

How those steep Catskill Mountain roads used to scare me. Sometimes today, when I ride in a limousine with its hundreds-of-horsepower engine, its powered hydraulic brakes, and its cruising speed of 70 or 80 miles per hour, I am just a mite homesick for the fun the family and I had in our little old "tin lizzie."

None of our other marvelous, modern gadgets has done so much to change our social and economic life as has the automobile. I often wonder if those who live 50 years from now will see as much difference between their age and ours as there exists between ours and that of 50 years ago. What do you think?

# CHAPTER NINE

# SPRINGS LIVE FOREVER

**E**ARLY ONE SUMMER MORNING, WHEN I WAS FIVE OR six years old, Father hitched one of the old farm plugs to the buggy, and Mother started with me and my brother Albert, who was a baby, for Grandpa's house. Mother's parents lived about 25 miles from our farm, but measured in terms of present-day means of transportation, it equaled about 200 miles with our plodding farm horse. I have traveled that same road many times in recent years, with a car, in a half-hour, but it took nearly all day for Mother to make the trip. It was so far, indeed, and such an undertaking, that Mother seldom saw her parents more than once or twice a year.

To pass the time and to keep us children from

whining, Mother sang and told us stories about what life was like when she was a little girl. At noon, we stopped in the shade by a roadside watering trough. Mother tied the horse and tied a nosebag over his mouth, filled with oats for his noonday meal. Then she unpacked our lunch, which we washed down with the almost ice-cold water that gushed from a spring in the roadside bank and flowed from a little wooden trough into the big watering trough.

That watering trough has been gone these many years, but the spring is still there and always will be. The countryside lost something when the watering troughs disappeared, in the march of progress, with the building of paved roads.

When our lunch was over, we resumed the slow and tedious journey to Grandpa's house. Toward the end of the trip, I would ask every few minutes, "How much farther is it, Ma?" But the hard trip was fully repaid by the affectionate reception we all got, although it seemed to me at the time that there was quite a lot of partiality shown to Albert because he was a baby. Maybe, though, that was just jealousy on my part. If there was any partiality, it was no doubt due to the fact that I had reached the age

where I was more devilish and troublesome than I was cute. There are times, I am sure, when members of my family and friends think that I have never outgrown that age!

Aside from the roadside spring on the way to Grandpa's house, the one I remember with most pleasure gushed out of the ground at the edge of the woods right next to where we had a crop of potatoes. The lot was on the back of the farm, a mile from home, so Father, an older brother, and I always had to take our lunch with us. Unless you have had the experience, you can't realize how long those work days seemed to a boy growing up Day Before Yesterday. We got up at 4:30 or 5:00 in the morning, drove in the cows from the night pasture, milked them, did the other chores, ate a big breakfast, and were in the field ready to work at 7:00, which is before most people today are even out of bed.

We worked steadily until noon, ate dinner, and rested a few minutes. How grateful I was for those few minutes to stretch out on my back and relax, until all too soon it was time to go back to work. From 1:00 until 4:30 or 5:00, we continued to work in the field; then someone drove in the cows from

This was my younger brother and myself when we were all "dolled up" to take the long trip (about 20 miles) to Grandpa's house.

the hill pasture. We did the chores all over again and at long last we were ready for supper, and soon after for bed.

You can well understand how a boy with that kind of a schedule had little time for deviltry. I guess the phrase "juvenile delinquent" hadn't been invented yet. At least I had never heard of it, and I know there was little of it in our neighborhood or in the nearby village.

But go back with me to that back-lot potato field. We dropped those seed potatoes by hand, and covered them with a hand hoe. When they came up, they were cultivated by a one-horse cultivator and then every hill had to be weeded and hoed carefully by hand. How I listened for the distant whistle of the passenger train that went down the valley over the hill just a few minutes before noon. How I watched that sun climb slowly to its zenith, indicating that it was time to eat. How I hated to be caught at the wrong end of the field at noon and have to hoe another row back again before I could rest and eat.

When finally noon did come, we went to the shaded spring at the edge of the woods, unpacked our dinner pails, and ate every crumb in them. What wouldn't I give for such an appetite now; but on second thought, what would I do with it? For if I ate now as I did then, I would be as fat as Mr. Richardson, a neighbor I knew, who weighed 400 pounds.

In the fall, we dug and picked those potatoes by

hand and stored them in the big bins in the farm cellar, or carried them in the lumber wagon to the railroad station five miles away, where they were shipped to market.

A year or so ago, I went back to that old potato field. It had grown up to brush and trees, so I had some difficulty in locating it. But I finally found that spring around which my father, brother, and I had eaten so many lunches and refreshed ourselves with the water from it so many times. There were a few leaves in the little basin, which had outlived its usefulness, but the flow of water from the spring was full and strong as it always will be. As Tennyson wrote about brooks, so it is with springs:

"Men may come and men may go,

But I go on forever."

As I lay flat to drink again the pure cold water, for a while it seemed to me that the years had rolled away. I was a boy again and had really found the "Fountain of Youth."

\* \* \*

One summer during the Second World War, our water supply failed on our farm, and we had a decision to make as to whether we would drill a well or pipe the water some distance from a hillside spring.

More for the fun of it than because I believed in it, I got a water witch or dowser to come with his stick with its two prongs to locate the best place in which to drill our well and make sure of a good water supply. He came with his stick (they were usually made of hazel or willow wood), and with the prongs of the stick grasped tightly in his hands, and with his arms extended in front of him, he walked slowly around and around the yard. Finally the stick turned down—right in the middle of the hard road that led into the yard, where it was practically impossible to drill a well. So I never had a chance to prove whether the dowser was right or wrong.

Skeptics would say that the turning stick is a subconscious reaction of the dowser's mind and no proof that water will be found at the place where it turns down. The dowsers have so much proof that they can find water that I am not at all sure myself who is right.

\* \* \*

Having decided not to drill a well when our water supply failed during the Second World War, we located a spring in a gully near the edge of the woods some distance from the house, and were faced with the tremendous job of digging a ditch from the spring to the house and barn. No machinery was available, so it had to be done with pick and shovel.

But we solved the problem. A few miles from the farm there was a German prisoner-of-war camp, and I made arrangements with the commander of the camp to use some of those German boys. They were the best farm help I ever had. Every morning we brought over as many boys as could fit in the car, taking them back to the camp at the close of the day's work. Because I was busy after the first day or so, Belle transported them without the least fear. They were just like her own boys, two of whom were in our Armed Forces. What workers those German boys were! How the dirt flew, and how cheerful and full of laughter they were.

When we noticed that they had brought little or nothing for their noonday meal, we took them into the house and loaded the table with heaps of plain food. I have never seen anyone eat the way those Germans did. No matter how much food the women put onto the table, there never was a crumb left when the boys got through.

Only one of the Germans could speak English.

He was a college graduate and I used to visit with him about Germany and the war. Like millions of other soldiers before and since who have fought the battles of the world, he wondered what it was all about and why it was necessary.

"Why," he said, "should we try to kill each other?"

This man told me, also, that several of the boys in the camp liked America so much that they wanted to stay here when the war was over. But sometimes the German boys were homesick. I found one of them once in a secluded part of the barn, his whole body shaking with sobs. I couldn't talk to him, but I knew what was the matter, so I put my arms around his shoulders and held him for a moment. Then he straightened up, gave me a pathetic little smile and went back to digging the ditch.

When the ditch was completed and the pipe laid and covered, the water from that spring started to flow to the house and barn and has never since failed, even during the summer of 1962, when there was the worst drought ever seen in this section.

\* \* \*

When you turn on a faucet and get all you want of either hot or cold water with a twist of your wrist,

Many believe that water witchers can locate an underground spring or well water with a dowsing stick. The operator grasps each prong tightly and when walking over water, the stick is supposed to turn down.

how many of you over 50 remember what a job it was to pump and carry water? In common with other farm boys, I have pumped water by the hour into the watering trough for the cattle and horses. I used to wonder how in the world any animal could hold so much.

It is said that cattle, when thirsty, can smell water from a considerable distance. I believe it. My uncle had a never-failing spring that supplied both the house and the barn with plenty of water even in the driest times. One of my neighbors wasn't so fortunate. He had to carry water for his cattle in a dry time almost every year. Apparently his cows were always thirsty. Frequently they made a nuisance of themselves by breaking out of their barnyard or pasture and visiting my uncle's place to drink from the big trough in the barnyard. It fell to the lot of one of my cousins to keep watch and drive the neighbor's cows away from their trough. She got exceedingly tired of the task, so one day she tied a tin can to one of the cow's tails. She began to run—the cow, not the cousin—and every time she jumped she banged her heels against the tin can; she went down the road faster, I suppose, than any cow has run before or since. After her, making close seconds, were all of her mates trying to beat her to the safety of their own yard. A little rough maybe, but it worked, for the cows never came back.

What a job it was to get that darn pump in the barnyard or the one near the house that supplied the water for the household thawed out and operating on a bitterly cold winter morning. I'll bet that no boy or girl today even knows what I mean when I say that pumps always had to be primed in the wintertime. As if it wasn't enough to pump water for the cattle until you were blue in the face, we boys used to have to pump and carry water to keep the big reservoir filled on the back of the old kitchen stove, fill the teakettle, and pump and carry all the water for the other household needs.

But let's come back to the springs that made it possible to have running water in both house and barn without pumping it. Not all of the watering troughs were on the roadside, of course, for almost every farm that had a good spring had the water piped from it to the house and to the barn or barnyard. Not only did that spring water in the troughs save a boy from the eternal pumping of water by

hand, but the troughs of water came in handy to dunk a setting hen in when she was more interested in producing a family than she was in laying eggs for Mother's grocery money. Watering troughs were also supposed to be a good place for a small boy to put a long horse hair in and have it turn into a snake, but although I tried and tried, I never could make the darn thing work.

On the farm where we lived at one time when I was small, there was a spring, the water from which was piped to a trough in the barn and to a round tub in a little alcove off the big farm kitchen. Although there was no faucet either at the barnyard or in the house, the water flowed from that spring fast and full and never failed, so that the water in both places was always fresh and sweet. That constant flow of the water in the kitchen could be heard through most of the house and it was a soothing, pleasant sound, good to sleep with and good to remember.

In the big cow stable on the farm which Belle and I worked when we were first married, there was a round watering trough or tub with a capacity to supply water for the 40-cow dairy. All the water we needed for that big dairy was piped to that trough from another, never-failing spring.

It was before the day of very many milking machines, and my brother Fay was helping me with the evening milking of our big dairy herd. Now Fay had a habit of sitting on the one-legged milking stool next to the cow, with a pail between his legs, and

The big outdoor kettle had many uses.

then, instead of milking, he would rub the nail of his forefinger across his upper lip while he dreamed of anything and everything except getting the milking done.

So, thinking I would wake him up, I grabbed a big force pump, used for throwing water in washing the buggy, stuck it in the watering trough, trained it on Fay dreaming away on his stool, then raised the handle of the pump and shoved it down hard. It threw a heavy stream of water squarely onto Fay amidships. He fell off the stool. What milk he had in his pail spilled, and then with a murderous yell he picked himself up and took after me. I didn't stop to argue, but ran for my life through the long cow stable, across the barnyard, and over the fence. I think I jumped that fence without touching it. As I raced down the slope of the pasture, a sizeable rock whizzed past me.

The milking must have been about done. If it wasn't Fay may have finished it, for I didn't dare show up at the house until I was sure things had simmered down.

* * *

I have always been thankful that I live in the Northeast, where we have so many springs. Much of America, particularly the prairie country, is not so fortunate and has to depend on wells. But as the Northeast might well be called "the land of springs," so many parts of the West could be called "the land of windmills" because windmills were used quite generally to pump the water out of the wells until the coming of the age of gasoline.

Friends raised in the West have told me that in many sections there was a windmill on every farm, and that the sight of one still grinding and groaning brings a nostalgic feeling to those who grew up with them.

Today it is indeed convenient to turn on the hot or cold faucet and get all the water you need, but as I drink it, often tasting heavily of chemicals, I wish I had the thirst from working in a hot hayfield and the opportunity to quench that thirst with the live, soft, sweet water of a spring.

# CHAPTER TEN

# WHEN WE TOOK TO THE WOODS

O N THOSE WINTER MORNINGS WHEN THE UNHEATED upper-chamber bedrooms were colder than Greenland's icy mountains, it was pleasant to dress by the round oak "settin'" room stove, but that stove and its brother, the kitchen range, were hogs for fuel.

Before I went to high school, and weekends afterwards, it seems as if I could never have a spare moment because I had to keep the big wood boxes filled—or saw, split, and pile wood to keep a supply ahead. That was one chore that boys who were raised in the South could thank their stars that they never had to do. Maybe we should have been thankful that we had the wood to cut. Friends who were raised in the prairie country, where there were few trees, have told me that they spent many weary hours picking up beef cow manure chips for fuel, and these friends always add how gosh-awful the stuff smelled when it was burned.

On many a cold winter Saturday morning, Mother packed a lunch for Father and me, and we traveled a mile or so to the wood lot to put in a day in renewing the wood supply. One of the fine skills lost now in most parts of America is one our fathers had in handling an axe and a cross-cut saw. Those two tools are almost as much responsible for settling America as was the plow. When you think of it, what a gigantic task it must have been to clear the forests of America!

For several years after the Civil War, Father worked as a lumberman during the winter. When the spring floods came, he helped to transport the logs, tied together in big rafts, down the Susquehanna River to Philadelphia. When the logs were sold, the crews walked all the way back home, perhaps to make another trip. As a result of Father's experiences in the woods, he could wield an axe better than anyone else I've ever seen. With each stroke biting deep and on the spot where he wanted it, he could fell a tree in a matter of minutes exactly where he wanted it to fall.

But Father used an axe little on a large tree if he had someone to help him with a cross-cut saw. Then he would use an axe only to make a deep gash on the side of the tree where he wanted it to fall, and then saw most of the tree through from the other side. If you want to know what hard work is, you should get down on your knees in the snow and help saw down a large tree with a cross-cut saw. I always worked well with Father because we were both long-armed; but it was not so with an older brother whose arms were short, because I always wanted to pull the saw through the log further than my brother could reach. We were constantly trading sarcastic remarks like, "I don't mind your riding the saw, if you wouldn't drag your feet."

Sometimes, no matter how skillful a woodsman was, a tree would fall on a shorter one and lodge there without coming completely down. Then it was a highly dangerous job to dislodge it and get it down the rest of the way. One of my father's brothers got a broken back when a lodged, partly-down tree suddenly broke loose and fell on him.

After a tree was felled, there came the tedious job of trimming off the smaller limbs and sawing the main stem into logs that could be handled on the skidways, from which they could be loaded on bob-sleighs and hauled to the sawmill for lumber or to the house to be cut up into firewood.

When noon came in the woods, we built a fire, heated our cold coffee, thawed out our frozen sandwiches, and had our lunch. If you have had a similar experience, you can understand how good that lunch tasted after that long cold work. When some of the young college students with whom I visit now claim that they have no appetite for breakfast or for some other meal, I wish they could have had the experiences of some of my generation who had to do chores two hours before breakfast, or work in the woods on a cold winter day.

Belle's father, who was a skilled woodsman in his early days, used to tell a true story about a man who was working with him in the woods one day in the winter. At noon, they built their fire and thawed out their lunches. When Mr. Stevens opened his dinner pail, he took out the upper section or the shelf on which was a big delicious piece of apple pie. He set the pie aside while he ate the rest of the meal, all the time anticipating topping off his lunch with that apple pie. But while they were eating, a winter bird flew overhead and by one chance in a million, he left a dropping squarely on that piece of pie. With a great yell of rage, Stevens jumped to his feet and went plunging off down through the woods in a futile attempt to wreak vengeance on the bird.

\* \* \*

As you ride in an airplane over the Northeast and some other parts of America, you are likely to conclude that the country is still well covered with woods. While there are many woodlands left, from an airplane they stand out in contrast to the larger, cleared fields around them. Unfortunately, except for the mountainous sections of the country, almost all of the good timber has been cleared, leaving only brush and second growth stuff.

The settlers, faced with the necessity of clearing the land as fast as possible, felled and burned the great virgin trees that would be worth a fortune today. Unfortunately, there has never been a consistent policy of replacing trees by scientific reforestation when the aging trees of a wood lot have been removed. This ruthless, wasteful policy, along with the inroads of insects and diseases that attack our beautiful trees like the elms and maples, is rapidly losing us one of America's most valuable and beautiful resources.

A well-kept wood lot can be one of the most valuable assets to the farm and to the whole community.

Not the least of those assets from the woods are the maple products in the northern sections of America where the hard maple grows. I well remember that early spring morning when Father hustled out to begin tapping the trees. The beautiful clear sky in the east gave promise of a warm, sunny day. The roofs of the barn and out-buildings were covered with a white frost. Some snow still lay on the ground. Father ate his breakfast with an absent-minded air, so we boys knew there was something on his mind. The time of freezing nights and sunny days had come, and sap was running in the hard maples.

Sure enough, before we had hardly finished breakfast, Father said, "Stir yourselves boys, we're going to get the sap buckets out, wash them, and start tapping the maples."

From then on, for the next two or three weeks, whenever we got sunny days preceded by frosty nights, the making of maple syrup and sugar was almost a night-and-day business on the old farm. But we loved it. It was the first outdoor job of the spring, and there was something about the whole operation that was fun, at least in retrospect.

Next to honey, maple products are the oldest known sweets in the North, wherever the hard maples grow. They were the only sweets known to the Indians and white settlers. The Indians made a deep gash in the hard maples and caught some of the running sap in a wooden bowl or gourd shell. Then they would evaporate the sap by dropping hot stones in it or by boiling it. Sometimes they let the sap freeze several times, each time taking off the ice and thereby getting a very thin syrup. Of course, the old processes of making syrup and sugar were very wasteful, but with a northern forest filled with maples, what did it matter?

Neither did the Indians nor the white settlers worry much about the cleanliness of the final product. A few years ago, I had a friend who insisted that dark maple syrup tasting of smoke and old leaves was the best kind. But not for me. High-quality maple syrup should be light in color, with nothing but the delicious taste of the maple itself—the nectar of the gods.

Carrying sap with a shoulder yoke.

Incidentally, we once had a neighbor who froze hard cider in the same way that the Indians made syrup, by repeatedly freezing it until the resulting, concentrated product made him and some of his friends yump and yump and yump.

The northern Indians used maple syrup in almost everything they ate, including their meat. They had nothing on another neighbor I once knew, who said, "If I can just get through the winter until maple syrup time and dandelion greens, I'll be good for another year." He, like the Indians, used syrup on all of his food, including his potatoes.

The early settlers in the North, where the hard maples grew, learned from the Indians how to make maple syrup and how to use it, but they soon improved the methods of making it. They used wooden buckets hung on the trees to catch the sap, and they evaporated it in big iron kettles slung on poles over an outdoor fire. I have made lots of syrup that way. Also, when I wanted to make a little for home use, I have tapped a few maples around the house and boiled the sap down on the kitchen stove, using up a sizeable wood pile and peeling the kitchen wallpaper off with the steam in the process.

When I was a boy, we bored two holes in the maples close together and inserted spiles made of sumac, with one end sharpened to fit the auger hole in the tree. With a small, red-hot iron, we burned the pith out of the sumac stem, making a round hole through it. Through this hole, the sap dripped into the wooden or tin buckets. We gathered the sap from the buckets, poured it into a big tub on the longsleigh, hauled it with the horses to the sap house, and stored it in tanks or tubs until we could boil it into syrup in the long rectangular vats set on brick arches over a roaring fire.

Later we were able to buy short and much better metal spiles. If the maple was a large one, we set two or three buckets to a tree. I can still remember how sore my stomach got from leaning against the bit or the auger to bore the hole into the tree for the spiles. It was a big job during the year, when there was any spare time, to gather the wood needed, like old fence rails and limbs from the woods, to feed the hungry maw of that furnace.

When the syrup was boiled as far as we could in the sap house, we poured it from the vats or pans into milk cans and took it to the house, where Mother boiled it on the kitchen stove to just the right consistency. Then it was poured into gallon cans ready for market. We used to sell hundreds of gallons of maple syrup for $1 a gallon. Now it costs $5 or $6.

The sap house was usually a ramshackle shanty, set, if possible, on a side hill, so that, with the storage tanks on the upper side of the house, the sap would run down into the pans, where it was evaporated.

The other day, in a museum, I saw a shoulder-carrying yoke—a wooden device that went around the neck and over both shoulders so that pails of sap, water, or milk could be carried by using each shoulder. We had an old neighbor who had a maple grove, who would carry sap with one of those yokes from his trees into the sap house.

Maybe I wouldn't think so now, because there really is much hard work even with modern equipment in the making of maple syrup and sugar, but when the weather was perfect so that the sap ran almost in a stream and we knew that the boiling must be carried on all night to keep ahead of the "big run," I was always more excited about it than about anything else that happened on the farm.

An older brother kept the sap boiling one evening during a sap run while the rest of us did the chores and ate our supper. Then Bill (a neighbor boy who had come to spend the night with me) and I rushed for the sap house. When I pulled open the door, the steam inside was so thick that I could hardly see my hands in front of me. I squatted down to get under the steam and made my way to where Fay, my brother, was sprawled on the long bench, taking it easy. After we got used to the steam and smoke, Bill and I took a dipper and got some of the thicker syrup from the front pan. When it was cool enough, we drank a lot of it. It was good—thin, sweet, hot, but laxative. For a spring tonic, it had Mother's rotten-tasting sulphur and molasses beaten all hollow.

Fay went to the house and left us to do the boiling. Every little while we would take down the sheet-iron, which served as a door to the furnace, and stuff more wood into the blazing fire. Later in the evening, several neighbor boys kept us company and we treated them all to dippers-full of the partly boiled syrup, while we talked lazily about the things that boys have talked about since the beginning of time, alternating the talk between the chores of stoking a fire and watching to see that the evaporation was going all right.

Some time during the evening, Father came up to the sap house, took a look at the storage tanks, and

When you worked all day tapping the hard maples for the first run of sap, using a brace and bit, you could have a mighty sore belly from supporting the brace with your middle, but it was fascinating to see the sap spurt from the newly bored hole.

said, "We'll have to keep her goin' all night, for we're sure to have a big run again tomorrow."

With some enthusiasm, we assured him that we would keep her boiling.

"All right," he said. "Watch it and don't let the pans run dry or the syrup run over."

Sometime along toward midnight, when we got hungry, we would put some eggs into the boiling sap, which tasted all the better because they were probably stolen from Mother's pantry.

Always, some time during the maple syrup season, there would be one or more maple-sugar parties in the neighborhood. You have missed something if you have never attended one of these parties or a good substitute—a molasses candy pull. For the maple-sugar festivities, you had to have several pans packed hard with clean snow. Then the new maple syrup was boiled to just the right consistency, so that when it was dropped by the spoonful onto the hard snow, it congealed into a soft candy not to be compared with any other sweet in the world. Almost equally as good was a saucerful of the thickened syrup, which you stirred rapidly until it became a soft sugar and would melt in your mouth while you rolled your eyes cross-eyed at your nose, savoring the wonderful taste.

But, like everything else, customs change and with the changes some of the old-time fun has gone. More important, the maples are rapidly disappearing and are not being replaced. Up and down the valley where I was raised, there was a maple grove on nearly every farm. Today, there are only one or two left, and the trees of these are showing their age.

Vermont, northern New York, and some other parts of the North are still producing large quantities of maple products, but unless more effort is made to plant new trees, a profitable and romantic rural industry will become a thing of the past. Can you who grew up in the land of hard maples visualize the American scene without the maples, with their glorious attire, in the fall? Without them, we will have lost a thing of beauty that never can be replaced.

# CHAPTER ELEVEN

# "MUSIC HATH CHARMS-"

With all of the opportunities to enjoy music that we have today, none of the younger generation can realize how starved most people were for music Day Before Yesterday.

Never will I forget the carpenter who lived with us one summer while he was building our new barn. When day's work was done and supper over, he would open a worn violin case and take his violin out as if it was just about his dearest possession—as indeed I am sure it was. I can close my eyes and hear him still, intently tuning the instrument before he was off with the merry old jigs and the ballads that have entertained the people down through the ages. How disappointed I was when he had finished and carefully put away his beloved fiddle.

In our house, when I was a small boy, sometimes there was a mouth organ which an older brother played, and there was a piccolo which he took along on a Sunday afternoon when he and I walked in the hills. When we got tired, we rested, and while I lay flat on my back, perhaps with my ragged straw hat over my eyes, listening to the shrill notes of the piccolo echoing across the valley, my brother would play "The Girl I Left Behind Me," "John Brown's Body Lies A'Mouldering in the Grave," or maybe "Dixie." It was nearer to Civil War times then, and as I listened I could almost see those columns of blue or gray-uniformed men, and hear the tramp, tramp, tramp of their marching feet.

\* \* \*

I have already mentioned some of the songs that Mother used to sing while holding my baby brother on her lap as I sat on a little stool by her knee. It is too bad that since the coming of so much recorded music, women don't sing like they once did.

In our home, we had one little musical instrument that I listened to by the hour. It was called an autophone. I'll bet you a dime you don't know what it was like. I haven't seen an autophone in years, but it was a small wooden instrument with a bellows pumped by hand, through which was run a long sheet of perforated paper. As the holes crossed the top of the bellows, the air escaping through the holes made the music.

Oh yes, I mustn't forget the jew's-harp, a small gadget which you played against your teeth and vibrated by twanging the metal tongue. Ever see one? If you couldn't play a jew's-harp Day Before Yesterday, you were just no musician.

\* \* \*

When I was small, an old soldier came to our house one day, who was a great curiosity to me because he had a wooden leg. This was Mr. Signor, and his business was selling parlor organs. What a great day it was when he unloaded that wonderful, bright, mysterious musical instrument and put it right into our parlor. It took Mother several years to pay for that organ by picking and selling blackberries and by saving her egg money.

Longfellow said, "A boy's thoughts are long, long thoughts," and mine were never longer than when sitting and dreaming in a little rocking chair in the parlor at twilight while Mother played the organ. Father had two favorite hymns which Mother played and sang frequently. After I learned to appreciate beautiful poetry, these hymns became my favorites also. The first was that grand expression of faith written by Cardinal John Newman:

Lead kindly light, amid the encircling gloom;
Lead thou me on!
The night is dark and I am far from home;
Lead thou me on!
Keep thou my feet, I do not ask to see
The distant scene;
One step enough for me.

The lines above often come back to me when I drive a car alone in the night, when one can see ahead only as far as the lights of the car. I know that if I keep going, the way will be lighted for me as I need it.

Sometimes, when troubles and sorrows seem too hard to bear, it is best to live only one day at a time and not try "to see the distant scene."

Nothing that was ever written is more comforting, more beautiful than my father's other favorite, Alfred Lord Tennyson's "Crossing the Bar." You know it, of course, but read it again now and sense the full meaning of every word:

Sunset and evening star
And one clear call for me!
And may there be no moaning of the bar,
When I put out to sea,
But such a tide as moving seems asleep,
Too full for sound and foam,
When that which drew from out the boundless deep
Turns again home.
Twilight and evening bell,
And after that the dark!
And may there be no sadness of farewell,
When I embark;
For tho' from out our bourne of Time and Place
The flood may bear me far,
I hope to see my Pilot face to face
When I have crost the bar.

* * *

From Colonial Days to the end of the nineteenth century, people fed their starved longings for music

97

The Old Brass Band. What music they made!

by attending singing schools. These were neighborhood affairs, usually held in the little country schoolhouse, with no accompaniment except a tuning fork to set the key. The singing school was led by a traveling teacher or sometimes by the neighborhood's own school teacher or the pastor of the country church.

The old-fashioned singing school has been succeeded by modern community singing, but somehow it is not at all the same. In a singing school, with its do-re-mi or do-se-do, there was a closeness of fellow feeling—of unity of the singers—that is lost in the larger groups when singing is only a preliminary to the real program. What matter if some of the voices were old or cracked, and others sang between the cracks! When the neighbors sang together in a singing school or around the parlor organ, animosities and problems were forgotten for the moment, and they were together in spirit like a family.

* * *

No one who knows me now would ever believe that I once sang in a village church choir, but I did sing a bass of sorts. But while I never had any illusions about the quality of my own singing, I had a friend who had a voice which could have made him famous.

This friend once told me the story about the choirs in the village churches which were not far apart. It was a beautiful Sunday morning with all the windows of the churches open. At the beginning of the services, the choir in the first church arose and sang "Will There Be Any Stars In My Crown?" Immediately following, the choir in the church down the street sang "No, Not One." Then the third church further down sang "Won't That Be Glory For Me?"

While we can poke a little fun at some of the old gals who sang too loud and the men who sang off-key,

I like to think of the uplift of the spirit and the new outlook on life and its problems that we received when listening to our friends and neighbors singing in the village choir.

* * *

It is said that the influences on our lives during our first 10 years are the strongest and most lasting that we ever receive. Be that as it may, I am sure that Mother's singing and playing on her parlor organ, and the influence of my two older brothers, one of whom played a flute and a piccolo, and the other a clarinet in a country band, gave me a love of music and a desire to play an instrument, however badly, which has lasted throughout my life. Unfortunately, my desire to play greatly exceeded my natural ability as a musician. However, there are few experiences that I would trade for those I had and the friends I made while playing in the village band.

One of my best friends in the band was Fred, who played the big tuba or bass horn, while I played the little piccolo. One of Fred's favorite tricks when we were playing was to catch my attention and then puff out his cheeks like a big bullfrog. Now, in order

This music box is not an autophone like Mother used to play, but it worked on the same principle.

to play a piccolo or flute, you have to pucker your lips, and every time Fred puffed out his cheeks, I would lose my pucker and my place in the music and have a deuce of a time trying to catch up again. Fred, who was a good musician, tooted away without barely missing a beat while he was deviling me.

But I got even! We were playing one Saturday night to a big crowd on the village green. When we stood up to play "The Star Spangled Banner," I quickly removed the loose seat of Fred's chair, which

was close to me. When he sat down, he jackknifed right through the bottom of his chair and almost to the floor, with his big horn on top of him. It was some time before the leader could restore order so that we could go on with the concert.

Wilson was another friend and comrade in that band, who played a French horn and played it beautifully. One time, during a recess when we were playing at a country fair, Wilson asked me if I wouldn't like to go with him to visit the fair midway. Not daring to leave our instruments on the bandstand, we took them with us. That was easy for me, for I always could take my piccolo apart and carry it in my pocket, but to carry a big horn was awkward. Wilson and I visited several sideshows, where our bright uniforms always enabled us to get a free pass.

Coming out of one of the shows, Wilson suggested that we make believe that we were kids again and take a ride on the merry-go-round. Suiting the action to his words, he started on a run and tried to board the merry-go-round before it had stopped. It was going faster than he thought and he was encumbered by his horn, so the merry-go-round threw him. For a moment all you could see rolling over and over on the ground was, first a man on top and then a shiny horn. Frightened for a moment, I ran to him, but he was picking himself up, unhurt. Neither was his horn damaged, but he was fighting mad and stalked off, his feelings not helped any by the hilarity of the large crowd that had come running when he fell. I am sure that the next notes that Wilson blew on the horn were sour indeed, if they were any indication of his injured dignity.

Because I have always been partial to good band music, it was a great privilege in my life when Belle and I were able to attend a band concert given by John Philip Sousa, the March King, and his famous band. It's good to know that Sousa was not only a musical genius, but that he was a real human being bubbling with fun, and as upright a citizen as they come. I never put one of Sousa's marches on the stereo without thinking of the time Belle and I heard him and his band in the Polo Grounds in New York City, playing the music, much of which was his creation, to one of the largest audiences I've ever seen.

So it is with life. No matter how sentimental or serious we may be, there is always need to offset it by humor and a laugh. Strange to say, pathos and humor are closely allied. A speaker or entertainer of great ability can often make the same audience weep and laugh.

It is fine, indeed, that the schools and colleges have taken up music and that so many young people have the opportunity to learn to sing and play. The beautiful music that these school and college orchestras and bands can play is truly marvelous, but I can't help adding that we lost something from the American scene when most of the village bands disappeared.

# CHAPTER TWELVE

# GENTLEMEN OF THE ROAD

IF YOU ARE OF MY GENERATION, I AM SURE YOU have daydreamed, as I have, of putting a few personal things in a small bundle, tying them on a stick and starting off on foot to see the world, leaving all cares and responsibilities behind you. Perhaps when you were young, you actually did run away, but probably not for very long. Few indeed are those who have not at one time or another been struck by that uneasy disease which we call "wanderlust." The only difference between an old-fashioned tramp and the rest of us is that *he* had the courage of his convictions to cut loose from all of life's complications and responsibilities.

One fall day when I was young, my father, one of

my older brothers and I were digging potatoes. Stopping to rest for a moment, we saw a stranger coming toward us. He gave us a name which I have forgotten, but we always called him "Shorty" because he was short and thin. His age was hard to guess, because life and its cares had seemed to have made little impression on him. When he approached us in the potato field, we knew that he was a tramp. But he surprised us, because he wanted to know if we would like some help, for we knew that most tramps would rather be caught dead than work. Father told Shorty that he would be glad to hire him.

It was late in the forenoon, so we asked Shorty if he had had breakfast. To this, Shorty replied, "No, not yet." In all the several years when Shorty came to our farm on his travels, no matter what the time of day, if we asked him if he had eaten, he would always reply, "No, not yet."

Shorty helped us for a week or so and then, just as suddenly as he had appeared, he left before daylight one morning without saying goodbye. Sometimes, he would even leave without collecting his wages.

When we offered Shorty a bed, he refused, saying, "I want no truck with soft things. I'll take the hay-mow." Worried that Shorty might set the barn on fire, Father warned him against smoking. Shorty was indignant. "Never smoked in a barn in my life! Know better'n that!"

Shorty was a little man with a twinkling eye and a grand sense of humor, reasonably well dressed, surprisingly clean, and with a fund of information that made us young people glad when he came and sorry when he left. So fascinating were Shorty's stories of the road and of all the interesting things he had seen or experienced that they made a farm boy who had never been anywhere want to leave the dull farm work and join Shorty in his endless wanderings.

Shorty was never afraid to tell a story on himself, and always, at the end he would laugh heartily whether his listeners did or not. He claimed that the following actually happened to him. He said he knocked on the front door of a house one day and a woman came to the door. Shorty told her he had not eaten for two or three days and that he was near starving. "You just don't know how hungry I am," he told her, and to prove it he dropped down on his hands and knees and began to eat the grass on the lawn. "If you're *that* hungry," the woman snapped,

My friend, the late Will McCullough, with his mule and buggy. Will was one of the first R.F.D. mail carriers and with this outfit, he was a welcome visitor at our farm where he stopped midway in his route to have dinner with us and to feed his mule.

"go right around to the backyard. The grass is two inches taller there!"

Although some farm women used to be afraid of the Knights of the Road, a true tramp would never harm anybody. He got blamed for a lot of crimes he didn't commit. Although tramps were not above taking a much-needed garment from a clothesline or a hen or two from the chicken house, they were reasonably honest. They got their food and clothing, such as they were, by begging, and a few of them, like Shorty, earned most of their own way. They belonged to the informal Brotherhood which had its unwritten by-laws, signs, and language all its own. We always gave the tramps something to eat, so we knew that on

104

post or barn near our home every tramp who passed would find a secret sign indicating that *our house* was a good place to stop and beg. Marked also were the places where there was an ugly dog, or where, otherwise, a tramp would not get a good reception.

In visiting with Shorty, he was sometimes hard to understand because of his brogue, and especially when he forgot that we didn't belong to the Brotherhood so that we didn't understand his strange vocabulary. I remember a few of those words.

If you were "bughouse" you were crazy. A "bull" was a policeman, also called a "finger" or a "flatty." A "fly cop" was a detective. "Dead" meant reformed; that is, you might just as well be dead as to take a steady job. A "dip" or a "grafter" was a pickpocket, not a real tramp. Anyone not a tramp was a "hoosier." A "hostile" was an unfriendly place for tramps. Hostile towns were well posted and known. "Pennsylvania salve" meant apple butter. "Punkin plaster" meant bread and butter. A "rube" was a farmer, and a "sucker" was a victim of both tramps and criminals.

During the first 100 years of American history, there was no tramp problem. When there was a surplus of workers in an eastern community, they migrated westward. There were always new lands to explore and plenty of work to do.

But with the coming of the automobile, the wheel of history turned again, and men like Shorty disappeared. Why? There are many reasons. The quiet old country roads have been replaced by modern highways and millions of whizzing cars. My friend Shorty would have no peace on them nor would he be permitted on them.

Incidentally, I have often thought how much more interesting a road or a street is when you are walking it and have time to observe all the details, instead of whizzing through it when riding in a car. Shorty, for example, knew infinitely more about the country through which he walked than anyone ever does now from riding. With all of our traveling, we are forgetting what America looks like, close up.

To be sure, there was always warfare between the tramps and the "harness bulls," which was what the tramps called the policemen, and there was warfare also between the tramps and the "brakeys," the brakemen who threw the tramps off the freight trains. But while the officers of the law and the railroad brakemen sometimes won a battle, they never won the war until the coming of the cars, state police, and the highway patrol.

Day Before Yesterday, a man out of work had no choice but to take to the road or go to the poorhouse. Now he has unemployment insurance or welfare relief.

In spite of hunger and cold, and the disrespect of those who worked for a living, Shorty and his kind walked the road in their lifelong search for happiness, which they always hoped would be at the end of the rainbow. Perhaps they found it as well as you or I—not over the hill but along the road.

* * *

Another class that we might call Gentlemen of the Road were the pack peddlers of the horse-and-buggy days. I wonder how many of you can remember them. The coming of the peddler was a real event in my young life. To know how fascinating a pack was when it was open on the sitting room floor, you have to know how little out-of-the-ordinary routine there was to brighten the life of a child and his mother on farms years ago. Almost always, the peddler would first take out some little trinket and present it to me. That was good salesmanship, because it broke down Mother's sales resistance.

Then, spread before us there were: doilies, lambrequins (a narrow strip of cloth to hang from a window or doorway or from a shelf edge), chenille pieces, table spreads, maybe a bedspread, needles, thimbles (with open end), thread, an assortment of wonderful buttons, and perhaps a blanket and snuff boxes. There were also handkerchiefs, mittens, and gloves.

No matter whether the purchase was large or small, or none at all, the peddler was always cheerful, finally gathering up his pack, shouldering it, and trudging along the road to the next stop. Some of the old peddlers finally graduated to become store owners and a few even became great merchants.

Tin peddlers also traveled the roads about the same time the pack peddlers did, but they rode instead of walking, driving either one or two horses. The tin peddler I knew had a bright-red, enclosed cart, drawn by one horse. Inside, and hanging to the outside of the cart, there was about every piece of tinware known at that time. There were teakettles, coffee and teapots, tin cups, pie tins, basins of all kinds and sizes, pails, sap buckets, wash boilers, and tubs. The tin peddler always carried a supply of small, round milk pans used by dairy farmers to raise cream before the days of shipping milk. It would be interesting to know how many of you remember those pans.

Many of the pack and tin peddlers were real characters. Some of them carried small musical instruments like jew's-harps and mouth organs, with which they could soften the hearts of both kids and adults with old tunes and ballads. Occasionally, there was a tin peddler who carried a much-loved fiddle. I don't know what I would think of his music now, but then it was more glorious than anything I had ever heard.

I don't remember that any of the country peddlers dealt much in harmful gossip, but many of them were full of news about what was happening on the next farm and in the next neighborhood at a time when people were starved for news. Sometimes they carried messages from one friend to another. I remember that Mother always looked forward to their coming, not only to see their merchandise, but to hear what was going on in the world.

Both the tin and pack peddlers lived off the country. That is, they ate and slept wherever mealtime or nighttime overtook them, usually exchanging some of their treasures for the farmers' hospitality. One tin peddler was in the habit of staying fairly regularly at my uncle's house. Usually, he was good for an evening of visiting and entertainment. But late one afternoon, he arrived after some neighbor had filled him with plenty of hard cider. Not wishing to have him bother my aunt, and not daring to let him sleep in the barn because he might set fire to it, my uncle found some excuse for seeing him on his way, carefully turning the team around so that the peddler, in the haze he was in, would not overturn the cart. A good hour later, when my uncle happened to glance out of the window, he saw the team still standing patiently in the driveway, just about where he had left it.

When my uncle went out to see what was the matter, the peddler roused himself from the high seat on his cart and said rather plaintively, "Mister, I'm still here because you took away the lines of my horses." Uncle reached up, unwound the lines from the whipstock where they had been within easy reach of the peddler, gave them to the old man, and he and his outfit rattled out of the yard.

After the pack peddlers and the tin peddlers came the grocery cart on the country roads. What a godsend it was to rural people not to have to drive miles every week to get grocery supplies for the family. But there really wasn't too much in the first grocery carts. When the Great Atlantic and Pacific Tea Company, starting their business with their country horse-drawn carts, first began business, they did not carry much at first except tea, coffee, and spices.

Later came the grocer like our friend, Frank Nixon, who had his grocery store in town but spent most of his time on the road with a fully-stocked grocery cart. I suspect that it was much more interesting to him and many others like him to travel up and down the country roads and visit with the housewives all along the way than it would have been to stand, day after day, behind a counter.

* * *

Another class of gentlemen who began traveling the road and who still do travel all our roads regularly in great number are the rural delivery mail carriers, or the R.F.D. men. Only now, they travel with automobiles.

Shortly after the turn of this century, when I first knew the mail carrier, he drove a horse and buggy. It is interesting to contemplate the changes in mail delivery in one man's lifetime. When I was a farm boy—about 10 or 12 years old—we got the mail, what little there was, once a week by my riding a horse, bareback, five miles to the village post office. A little later, when we moved from that particular farm over the hill to a new valley and a new life, we got the mail every day from a neighboring farm kitchen. This kitchen served as a post office. The mail came up the valley by stagecoach from a large village, 10 miles away. Then came the big change. Congress established the rural free delivery (R.F.D.) mail service, which was and is one of the finest services rural people have ever had.

After sorting the mail in the village post office, Mr. Will McCullough, our first rural mail carrier, started with his horse and buggy on his long journey to visit every rural home on his route. Arriving at our place about noon, with his journey nearly half-covered, Will would put his horse in our barn to rest a while and be fed. Then he would come into the house to eat with us around the big table in our family kitchen.

How we enjoyed visiting with him while we broke bread together! A well-read man, Will could discuss current events, and he brought to us the personal news of our friends and neighbors, but he never spoke a word of malicious gossip. Will delivered the mail for a good part of a lifetime—first by horse and buggy, then by graduating to a car. In all those years, traveling on the dusty and muddy roads of spring and summer, and over the snowdrifts by horse and cutter in the wintertime, I can't remember that he ever missed more than a day or two. No matter what the weather, the mail had to go through! And what an event the daily delivery of the mail was in the often uneventful life of rural people! The distance Mr. McCullough covered in a lifetime, traveling six days a week every week in the year, except for a short vacation, would have carried him many times around the world.

I'm strictly a modernist, but there's a glamour about the old days and the old ways when the world was smaller and moved more slowly. I don't want to go back, but I would like to sit on the old front porch once again the way we used to at the close of day and listen to the peddlers' stories and their music, or visit again around the kitchen table, and hear the murmur of voices of those I loved who have long since gone.

# CHAPTER THIRTEEN
# WOMAN'S WORK WAS NEVER DONE

Oᴺᴇ ᴍᴏʀɴɪɴɢ ᴡʜᴇɴ ɪ ᴡᴀs ɢʀᴏᴡɪɴɢ ᴜᴘ, ᴡʜᴇɴ ᴛʜᴇ spring light in the eastern sky foretold a sunny day, Mother got a gleam in her eye and an absentminded manner that indicated that something was afoot. Father and we boys soon found out that there was. Mother had decided to start spring house-cleaning and it was the barn or the doghouse for us.

From that time on, for the next two weeks, we menfolks knew that we might just as well resign ourselves to Mother's short temper, to taking sketchy meals where and when we could, to freezing on cold mornings because the "settin" room stove had been taken down.

How I hated to see that round oak living room stove come down. To be sure, it ate wood like a hog gulps down swill and I knew that until fall came, I would not have to spend my Saturdays on the business end of a crosscut saw nor would I have to lug in from the woodshed armful after armful of wood and pile it behind that stove to feed the brute. But all the same, a bright day or two in March was a liar and a cheat for there were sure to be many more bitter cold days when the wind howled down the hills and the house would be cold as an icebox. Those cold mornings during house-cleaning time were when a shivering farm boy grabbed his clothes from the floor where he had shed them the night before and made a break for the warm cow stable.

After moving the stove out into the back kitchen and putting a cover over it for the summer, you had to get down on your knees with a tack-puller (Did you ever see one?) and go entirely around the whole room, prying out the tacks, nailed into the carpet every few inches, that held the wall-to-wall carpet.

Pulling the tacks was nothing to the job that came later. After lifting and lugging the carpet outdoors, we finally got the thing astraddle of the clothesline in the backyard. Then a boy had to whip it and whip it to get the dust out until he felt like whipping his

best friend. Finally, after he had beat the carpet about three times longer than he thought was necessary, he lugged it back into the living room, but not until Mother had scrubbed the bare floor until it shone.

Once every few years, while the carpet and the furniture were out of the room, Mother would paper it (the room, not the carpet). No hired outside help from a paperhanger for her! There was no money for that. She hung the paper herself after hours of pouring over mail-order sample paper catalogs. To prepare for the job, Mother made up a pan of paste, a mixture of flour and water. Then she laid each strip of paper across the kitchen table, daubed it with paste, and, standing on a stepladder, put the paper on the walls and ceiling. When she got through, the paper matched perfectly—as good a job as I have seen modern paperhangers do.

Did you ever hang paper? Don't try it unless you are experienced or have help. Once, just once, I tried papering a room. I thought if a woman could do it, I could. So I trimmed the edges off the rolls, made the paste of flour and water, slopped some of it on the strip of paper and started up the stepladder with it and stuck the top of the strip where I thought it should go. But that paper had different ideas. I started working down the strip, but when I got near the floor, the whole strip rolled down on top of me. Then, beginning at the bottom of the strip, I started all over again, working up. No soap! The paste had partly dried; the strip was dirty and torn—but why go on? Is there anything more devilish sometimes than the devilish perverseness of inanimate objects?

Finally, with the clean carpet all tacked down again, the pretty clean paper on the walls, we cleaned and moved back into the living room Father's favorite rocking chair with its colorful cushion, back pad, and tidy. (I still have it.) Moved back also were the comfortable old couch and the rest of the furniture. Then we washed the windows, doing an extra special job on the big bay window. That bay window held Mother's beautiful flowering begonias, her geraniums which were just beginning to open their buds to the spring light, and her many other house plants. On the big living room reading table, we set the large Rochester kerosene light, which had been shined up, and we piled the table with magazines, including copies of *The Youth's Companion* and the farm paper, *American Agriculturist*.

I recall my lying on that living room couch and watching the shadows on the wall from that Rochester light, with its green shade, as I drifted off to sleep to the murmur of the voices of my family or friends as they visited around the round oak stove or the reading table.

When we walked into that living room, all shiny and smelling of its cleanliness, even we boys had to admit that, while house-cleaning was an ordeal, maybe it was worth it. At least we would have admitted it if we hadn't known that the process had to be repeated for every room in the big farmhouse. The bedding and the mattresses of each bed had to be lugged out of the bedrooms, the bedding washed, and the beds thoroughly cleaned.

I had an uncle who, when he was young, like all other farm boys of his time, hated like all get-out to have house-cleaning time come, and he had reason to remember one particular time. Like me, he had the habit at bed-time of going into his room without a lamp. He'd let his overalls slide to the floor, kick off his shoes, and jump into bed. But alas and alack, his mother—with that fatal tendency of all women to change everything all around ever so often—had put the bed in another corner of the room. My uncle gave one leap for his bed and landed squarely on the bare floor!

* * *

When my mother died in 1937, there was in her house a three-quarter size rope bed on which she and my father had slept a good part of their lifetime. The bedstead had no slats but had knobs on the side rails to hold the rope, which was criss-crossed both ways across the bed, an old-time substitute for springs.

One of my early recollections of house-cleaning time is seeing Mother tightening up the ropes of that bed, which had stretched and sagged during the year.

Of course, there were no modern mattresses on those old-time rope beds. They were made comfortable—or reasonably so—by ticks filled with straw. If left too long without refilling, the ticks became hard and lumpy, and the would-be sleeper had to manage to dispose or repose himself around the many lumps. At house-cleaning time, we carried the ticks with their old straw to the barn and refilled them. If you were "finicky" about the bed you slept in, you sometimes put a feather bed over the straw mattress. This was

good on a cold night after you got the darned thing warmed up.

When house-cleaning was over, it was a joy to settle into the old routine again, eat regularly, sleep in the nice clean beds—and especially, to get Mother back to her own sweet, everyday self again.

If you ever catch me talking or dreaming about the good old times, just remind me of spring house-cleaning as it used to be. I'll take the modern way every time, with all of its labor-saving household equipment that helps the women keep their homes clean every day without breaking their backs and disrupting the whole family in the spring.

* * *

Recently, when I saw the hot water pouring into our new automatic washer, without our doing a thing about it except to turn on a faucet, I thought about how difficult washdays were in those days not so long ago.

How I used to hate Mondays. At breakfast, if we boys didn't know it was washday in any other way, we certainly knew from the absent-minded glitter in

The family did most of their living in the kitchen because it was such a pleasant place in which to be.

Old-time cooking and other kitchen utensils. How many can you name?

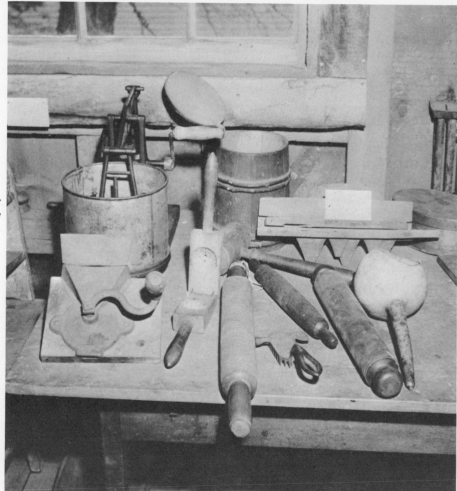

Mother's eyes. That look meant business. She built a roaring wood fire in the kitchen range, then ordered us to carry water from the pump in the front yard to fill the big wash boiler on the top of the stove.

When the water was hot in the boiler, Mother set two big washtubs on a bench, dipped the water from the boiler into one of the tubs, dumped in some home-made soft soap or perhaps some commercial stuff called "9 o'clock Tea." Do you remember it?

If you have ever had any experience scrubbing clothes on a washboard, you know how easy it was, if you didn't keep your knuckles well protected by the clothes, to scrub the skin off, especially after your hands had been soaked in the hot water. No wonder women's hands were worn and the knuckles enlarged. Then, after the clothes had been scrubbed clean, they had to be rinsed, blued, and wrung out as dry as possible either by hand, or, if a woman was lucky, with a wringer.

The dirtiest clothes were put back into fresh hot water in the boiler and boiled. Finally, after the many long and tedious processes, the clothes were hung out to dry. Summer or winter, they had to be hung on the long clotheslines out-of-doors. Did you ever have the experience of taking down a line of frozen clothes in bitterly cold weather? Remember how the kitchen would grow cold and damp as the frozen clothes slowly thawed out? In the warm bright, sunshiny days of summer, Mother used to spread some of the clothes on the green lawn to "bleach out" in the sun. How fragrant those pieces of laundry were when they were gathered up and brought into the house.

Add it all up, one wonders how women with a large family ever survived the ordeal of washday. Some of them didn't. Unfortunately, some still have to wash by hand, but many now have the magical machines which can be set for the washing and rinsing cycles while Milady goes about her house doing other work. And many men now do their part by taking the washing to the modern automatic "wash'n" shops.

At home, we never had running water or automatic hot water, but in later years we did get a contraption which was supposed to get the dirt out by suction, as a boy wearily pumped the thing back and forth. That gadget was followed by a so-called washing machine which was cranked by hand, for hours it seemed, while it whirled and sloshed the clothes back and forth inside the washer.

Wringers also took some of the hard work out of washing, but there was always the same amount of water to pump and to lug, and always the clothes had to be hung outdoors to dry. It was not until electrical power was developed that women got the marvelous automatic washers and driers which make modern washing as different from what it was only a few years ago as day is from night.

By the way, do you remember how women used to ride along a country road and slow up to look at a full line of clothes? They could tell you what kind of a family lived there, how many there were in the family, and what kind of a housekeeper the woman of the home was. The evidence was all on the clothes-line.

The long row of diapers told of a new baby and probably a tired and harrassed mother. Also in evidence would be Pa's old faded pants, his work shirts, long-johns, and socks. The number of children in the family was indicated by long or short assortments of boys' and girls' clothes in various stages of "hand-me-downs." And perhaps, tucked away modestly almost out of sight, were a few of the more intimate and unmentionable things that Mothers and sisters wore and that boys were not supposed to know anything about—but did!

Can you think of many things more tragic than to have that long-overburdened line of fresh clothes give way to fall in the dirt or mud on the ground so that the work had to be done all over again?

Tuesday was always the day when Mother ironed the big washing. Although I had to lug water for the washing until I was blue in the face on wash day, I was not considered old enough or maybe smart enough to iron, and with one exception I never tried to learn. That exception was on a Tuesday, when Mother had to be away from home. Thinking that I would give her a pleasant surprise when she returned, I built up a big fire in the kitchen range, heated up the flatirons, hauled out the clothes basket, heaped full of washing done the day before, and set about the ironing.

Mother's ironing board was a cloth-covered long board, which she usually laid across the table when she started her ironing. But why bother with that awkward board when the table itself was handier.

So I spread each garment as I ironed it on the bare dining-room table, which was just about Mother's only piece of nice furniture. After a little while, a peculiar burning smell filled the room, and on investigation I found that I had scorched the table-top with my too-hot irons, as well as some of the clothes. Of course, I hastily discontinued all operations, but when Mother came home—well, let's stop the story right there. The memory is too painful even now to put into words.

When I see Margaret doing the ironing with a beautiful electric steam iron, I often think of those irons that women once used. Mother had three or four of them on the hot stove, so she could trade frequently for a hot one as she ironed. Of course, it was difficult to regulate the temperature. But in spite of the boiling-hot kitchen and the need to stand on their feet for hours to do their ironing, many women took great pride in pressing clean clothes and putting them away in bureau drawers and linen closets.

* * *

The other day, when I watched Margaret give a thorough cleaning to several rooms in our house in just a short time with a modern electric vacuum cleaner, I thought of the tremendous job Mother and later Belle had of keeping a large house clean with nothing but a broom and maybe an old-fashioned "duster." As far as that duster was concerned, I am sure all it did was lift the dust from one place and let it settle somewhere else.

How many of you remember those brand-new brooms with their shiny handles, which a tin peddler carried on top of his cart? It was a real event when we got a new broom, for it is literally true that "a new broom sweeps clean"—at least, better than the old one. One of my grandmothers didn't even have a broom in the house. Instead, she sent Grandpa to the woods to get some short hemlock boughs which she tied to the end of a slit stick and made that do for a broom.

* * *

It was quite the general practice in the families in our neighborhood, including our own, to set the table for the next meal immediately after washing and drying the dishes. A properly set table, in addition to the regular dishes and knives and forks, always included the standard fixtures of a sugar bowl, pepper and salt shakers, and a caster, which was a revolving gadget in which there were a set of six little bottles of vinegar, pepper sauce and other commonly used supplementary food seasonings. When you wished to use one of these bottles farthest away, you revolved the caster until it came around where you could reach the desired one. A boarding-house wag suggested once that it would be nice if the whole center of the table on which was placed all the food could be revolved just like the caster. Then it would be *easy* —just as the boarder on the other side of the table was helping himself to the last piece of pie—to revolve the table quickly so as to bring the pie around to you. When our table was set with the plates and cups all turned down, a mosquito netting was spread over the whole table to protect the dishes from the flies.

One rainy day, when I had more energy than I knew what to do with, I began teasing an older brother who was reading and minding his own business. Finally, enough was too much for him, so, dropping his paper, he started to chase me around and around the table. I caught my foot in the netting, which hung too close to the floor, thereby hauling all of the dishes off onto the floor with a tremendous crash.

Brother disappeared rapidly out of the kitchen door; and Father came charging out of the sitting room. He took one startled glance at the wreck and then the race around the table began again, only now it was my father after me instead of my brother. Impeded by the mess of broken dishes on the floor, running was difficult, but finally, after two or three desperate rounds, I, too, dashed out of the door and disappeared for all the rest of the day.

That's the nearest I ever came to a licking from my dad. But Mother more than made up for it. There is no knowing where I would have landed if she hadn't.

Our cousin, Margaret Roe, tells a story about a dear old lady who lived in Brooktondale, where Margaret was born and brought up. The lady was a perfectionist and took great pride in keeping her house immaculate.

One Sunday, she and her husband came home from church and had dinner. Then her husband said, "We're so tired, why don't you leave the dishes until after we have had a good nap?"

While it went against her instincts, the lady packed the dirty dishes into the dishpan but she could think of no place to hide them until she thought of the sweet corn patch in the garden. So she took the pan of dishes and hid them between rows of corn.

Then the doorbell rang and company came to call. After a while, the lady's husband said, "I've got sweet corn much higher than knee-high on the fourth of July. Come out and see it!"

Not satisfied with standing at the edge of the garden, the husband stepped into the corn to show how high the corn was. Lo and behold—there was the pan of dirty dishes belonging to just about the neatest woman in Brooktondale.

I can imagine what that woman said to her husband when the company was gone—even if it was Sunday!

With a family of four boys, my mother had her heart and hands full taking care of us and doing all of her housework without outside help. For some reason, I was the one forced to help her, and one of the jobs which I hated was washing dishes. If you men never had much experience with the job, you have no idea of the deadly monotony of washing and drying dishes, three times a day, seven days a week, 365 days a year for a lifetime.

Belle used to make our two oldest sons, Donald and George, wash the dishes occasionally. Usually, it was more trouble to get them to do the job than it was for her to do the work herself. One night, after some argument about it, they cleaned up the dining room and kitchen in spic-'n-span order, but the next day, when she started setting the table, Belle noticed that quite a few of her dishes were missing. Puzzled, she started hunting, and finally found the missing ones well hidden in the laundry tub—dirty, of course.

We have a couple of cousins whose job it was, when they were little girls, to wash the dishes. Naturally, they got tired of it and so devised a little scheme of hiding for a while in the little out-house until they were sure their mother had done the dishes. She soon was wise to their little racket. So one boiling hot day, she slipped out and locked the little house from the outside. Then she finished the dishes and went about her other duties until the middle of the afternoon, when she let the culprits out. After that, they washed the dishes.

Some time ago, influenced by the experience of our friends, we bought a mechanical dishwasher. With the machine, it is nice to rinse and stack the dishes out of sight, turn on the switch and go away, leaving the dishwasher to do the work.

But you know something? There's no romance about a mechanical dishwasher. I sort of like the old-fashioned kind of dishwashing because I like to think of the gently whispered nothings that went back and forth between the girl and her sweetheart as she washed and he dried the dishes while her Pa and Ma were out of sight and out of hearing in the old "settin'" room.

We know a mother with a teen-age daughter. This mother says that she wouldn't give up the opportunity to get close to her daughter while they do the dishes together after the evening meal. They visit about what happened during the day and the mother says there is something about that shared work which makes it easier for them to talk, woman-to-woman.

Still another mother with daughters has always made it a practice to have something educational and worthwhile to talk about as they visit together doing dishes. A lady told me that when she was young, she and her sisters used to have real fun giggling together while they washed, dried, and put away the dishes. They did a lot of singing and harmonizing and, she admits, they occasionally threw some of the dish-water at one another. I suspect that this experience is better in retrospect than it was when it happened.

* * *

One of the difficult tasks in keeping a house clean and sanitary, especially on the farm, was fighting flies and mosquitoes.

Mosquitoes and flies have pestered people from time immemorial. I have often wondered how the settlers contended with them, for they had never heard of screens. The settlers did have one answer to the problem. They shut their doors and windows airtight, even during the hottest nights, because they thought the night air was poisonous. They were right, too, in one way. The air itself was all right, of course, but when their unscreened windows were open, in came the mosquitoes carrying malaria, one of the worst diseases of pioneer life in many sections of America.

No matter how good your screens were or how hard you tried, it was impossible to keep all the flies out of the house, particularly in the fall, when the weather began to grow cold and when the old kitchen smelled so nice of the canning, pickling, and cooking. Mother, and millions of other rural women, fought flies tooth and nail a good part of their lives. One of her methods was to take the stiff paper of a flour sack, cut it into strips, tie the strips to a stick

121

or part of a broom handle, then with several of these weapons, and with the aid of us boys, she opened the screen door and, starting from the back part of the room, flailed the air vigorously until we had chased the flies out.

Then, too, there was that old-fashioned sticky flypaper. Remember it? Our old tomcat did, I am sure, until the day of his death. He had a bad habit of jumping on the table when he thought we were out of the room and no one was looking. Mother used to clear off the big kitchen table and spread a sheet of flypaper on it. Old Tom, up to his usual tricks, jumped onto the table and landed right in the middle of the flypaper with all four feet. One of the funniest things I have ever seen was watching that fool cat roll off the table attached to the flypaper, race madly around and around the table and around the room, stop frequently to paw at the paper, and get it off one paw only to have it stick fast to another one. Finally he made a dash for the door, which I opened, and out he went, flypaper and all. It was hours before Tom came slinking back, a sadder and, I am sure, a wiser cat, for we never knew him to get on the table again.

You don't have to be old to remember the narrow strips of sticky flypaper which were suspended from the ceiling. They caught their share of flies, too.

How many, many times I have heard women say apologetically, "Oh, I am just a housewife." How wrong that point of view is! To be sure, it is more or less true that "A woman's work is never done," but there is no other trade or profession so important as making a home. It is the keystone and foundation of our society and our happiness.

# CHAPTER FOURTEEN

# I'LL TAKE THE OLE SWIMMIN' HOLE

THERE IS A GENERAL FEELING AMONG OLDER PEOPLE that we Americans have grown soft with luxury; that we are smothering, so to speak, in our own feather beds. But with the trials and tribulations that people had Day Before Yesterday, there was also a lot of fun, including the ole swimmin' hole, a welcome substitution for the Saturday night bath.

On a summer day recently, I went back to the neighborhood where I spent most of my boyhood. Leaving the car, I made my way through brush and tall weeds to the bank of the creek to the swimmin' hole that I knew as a boy. It didn't look much like it used to. Old scenes are disillusioning and never the same to an adult as they were when he was young, and it is always saddening to try to turn back the clock. When I swam that pool, a pleasant meadow stretched away from it to the barns of a neighbor. Today, the meadow has grown to brush. The creek itself seems smaller than it once was, and the swimmin' hole has filled up so that the water is now only a foot or two deep.

I sat down on the bank and thought of the fun we used to have there on a warm summer afternoon. We could always be sure, especially on Sunday, that there would be 15 or 20 boys from nearby farms, splashing in that pool or drying themselves in the sun. Now, I don't believe there are more than five boys or young men in that whole neighborhood. Those who do live around there are not interested in swimming in the nearby creek. Instead, they jump into their cars and drive to a lake or some public pool. But I wouldn't trade the companionship, the complete lack of inhibitions, and the fun that we used to have in that creek on a Sunday afternoon for all the modern swimming places there are!

Some of you will remember how you raced to get your clothes off so you would not be the last one in the water, and have others call out some insult. Bathing suits? Not on your life! I wouldn't have known what one was if I'd seen one. Of course people *did* wear them—but not in the ole swimmin' hole. Take one look at the pictures of bathing suits worn by both men and women on the beaches Day Before Yesterday, and you'll wonder why those who wore them didn't sink like a chunk of lead when they got into the water.

What a sense of well-being a fellow had after spending a warm afternoon in a swimming hole, alternating the swimming with drying in the sun on the gravelly beach. I had an older brother who used to swim with us sometimes. He was a practical joker, so none of us ever missed the opportunity to get back at him. One day, when there were only two or three of us in the swimmin' hole, my brother was the last one to get out. When he was not looking, another brother and I stole his clothes, which he had dropped off him before he started to swim. We took the clothes to the house, which was not far from the swimmin' hole. In between, there was good coverage of brush and trees until one reached the big backyard. When we got to the house, we found Mother visiting with some neighbor women under the shade of a tree in the backyard.

Putting brother's clothes in the house, we sat down to await developments. We didn't have to wait long.

Suddenly, a long white figure, without a shred of clothing on, emerged from the woods and with a great yell rushed across the lawn and disappeared into the house. I don't think he saw the women until it was too late to retreat. Later, we listened to a good strong lecture from Mother, but it was worth it.

As I sat on the shore of that old creek the other day, memories of the boys and young men who had gathered with me there came swarming back. There was Arthur who became wealthy as a real estate operator; his brother, George, who now lives in California; Roger, my boyhood chum, who became a famous doctor; Harry, Burt, and a dozen others, all of whom went forth from that neighborhood to be successful men and good citizens. Now, most of them are gone— gathered, perhaps, around an ole swimmin' hole on a warm and sunny afternoon "Somewhere Else."

\* \* \*

There used to be a city ordinance in Philadelphia against taking a bath. It was claimed even by some doctors in those days that bathing was weakening. Water was for drinking purposes only, and sometimes not even that, if something stronger was available.

I have a friend who claims that water rusts your insides. Now that ordinance would have suited a farm boy just fine before the days of universal showers and bathtubs. That Saturday night bathing chore was a real ordeal. Getting a bath in the summertime was all right because you could wash in the creek, but in the winter it was something else again. On Saturday night, you had to get a good fire going in the kitchen range. Then you pumped and carried the water, filled up the reservoir on the stove, and perhaps also the big wash boiler. When the water was hot enough, you dumped some of it into the big washtub in the middle of the kitchen floor, shed your clothes, and started in. When I was small, Mother kept sticking her nose into my business by coming into the kitchen during the bathing process to make sure I hadn't skipped a lot of area. She also made sure that none of us lazy boys used the same water as had the previous one.

There was one time, however, when I was glad to get that bath. That was when I had been "tailing" or "riding the elephant" back of the threshing machine when we were threshing barley. After some hours of doing that job, I was so black that even Mother wouldn't know me, and the sharp barley beards—remember them?—had worked down my neck till they seemed like a thousand devils pricking me.

No, we didn't spend Saturday night at the movies. There were no movies. It took the whole evening to make sure that all the family would not have to join the "Army of the Great Unwashed."

\* \* \*

When I hear or read the soap advertisements with their claims of what they will do to milady's complexion, I think of the soft soap we used to make and use when I was a boy. It would get the dirt off you all right, but if you weren't careful, it would take an arm off, too. Talk about milady's complexion—that homemade soft soap, if well rubbed in, would take the hair right off a cast-iron bulldog!

Remember how it was made? All winter, the folks saved the wood ashes from the stoves until they had a big barrel full of them. Then they set the barrel, end up on a small platform. Holes were drilled in the bottom of the barrel, then a little straw and two or three bricks were put into the bottom so that the little holes wouldn't get plugged. When the barrel was full

126

Every night during the long winter it was the boys' job to fill the wood boxes for both the stove and the kitchen range.

of ashes, we poured water on top. After a while, the water soaked down through the ashes and ran out the holes in the bottom where we caught it. The resulting product is called lye, and the apparatus for making it is a leach.

During the winter, Mother saved garbage—particularly that which contained any fat, like leftover soup, remains of a boiled dinner, offal from animals—almost anything, in fact, with fat, that ordinarily would be thrown away.

At last, on a spring day, we started the final operation of making soap. A big kettle was suspended from an arch over an outdoor fire. Into the kettle, Mother put the lye, and into the lye went that disgusting mess of garbage that she had been collecting for months. Some dairymen, and especially their wives, complain now about the awful smell from grass silage, but it is attar of roses compared to the smell given off by the boiling mess of lye and garbage. No other smell in my experience can equal that awful stench. How Mother ever stood it, I will never know. Maybe it was because she had to, but the rest of us found something to do as far away as possible.

When the mixture had boiled enough, Mother ladled it into the soap barrel, straining it through a porous cloth to keep out the pieces of garbage. After pouring in some more lye, Mother at last had her soft soap. Sometimes the mixture was boiled longer so that it would congeal into hard soap.

Good enough in summer but a little rugged at —10°.

I haven't seen any homemade soap in many years. Moreover, I don't want to. No wonder Mother complained about our dirty ears! It was too risky trying to wash them with that soap! As the years passed, we stopped making homemade soap and bought what we needed at the store; but doll it up as you will, advertise it to the skies, I will always be suspicious of soap.

Some years after Mother stopped making soft soap, she began buying big boxes of various kinds of soap, wholesale, from the Larkin Company. She got a box frequently, selling the surplus to the neighbors so that she could get the premiums that came with each box. From these premiums, she could get a piece of furniture, a cooking utensil, or some other prize. Hundreds of women did the same thing, so the Larkin Company can be credited with gladdening the hearts of many women with good furniture which they otherwise would not have had.

While I'm on this subject of washing, it is a good time to remind moderns of the blessings of bathrooms which we now all take for granted. We had none when I was a boy, nor was there one in the whole neighborhood or in the village over the hill. In most country homes, water had to be obtained from pumps. And even if there had been running water, there would have been no electricity with which to heat it. So it has not been many years since everyone has had to depend on the "little house out back." Some of those little houses had holes to fit every member of the family, large or small. Many of them were papered with old newspapers or pictures from which many a farm boy, including myself, received some education by reading and rereading them and the mail-order catalogs. But even though those little houses were fixed up as comfortably as possible, they still were

The saw-buck and buck-saw have driven more boys off the farm than anything else, with the possible exception of the hand hoe.

128

places to dread in the wintertime, especially at night.

When visiting with a friend about his experiences when he was a boy on a North Dakota farm, he told me of having to get out of a warm bed in the middle of the night and make a trip to that awful place outside, with the temperature 40 degrees below zero. "Grandpa and Grandma," he said, "were sometimes spared the ordeal on a cold night by the use of commodes and thunder mugs—but not the youngsters."

I said to him, "Probably experiences like that, particularly when men and women were old, shortened their lives." But my friend replied, "That's true for the old, but not for the young. The work and the endurance required to live in those times toughened a boy and girl and gave them the courage to withstand whatever came later in life."

# CHAPTER FIFTEEN

# WHAT WE "ET"

**I**F THERE IS ANYTHING THAT IRRITATES A WOMAN, it is to have her husband brag about his mother's cooking. As a matter of fact, the chances are that his mother's cooking was no better than his wife's. In fact, both men and women are misled, as they grow older, about how their food tastes because they do not have the appetites and the keen taste-buds of their youth.

Although it is no fault of today's home cook, there were some foods that actually *were* better than they are now because they were home-cooked and baked, and their goodness had not been processed out of them by modern manufacturing. Take homemade bread for example. What tasted better and *was* better Day Before Yesterday than a big slice from a well-browned and crusted loaf of homemade bread fresh from the oven, spread thick with homemade butter, and maybe sprinkled with brown sugar or touched lightly with maple syrup or New Orleans molasses? As an old Scotch lady, a neighbor of ours in my boyhood, used to say when she gave me a big slice of bread and butter with brown sugar, "It'll stick to your ribs, boy; it'll stick to your ribs."

But now I must spoil that picture a little with the reservation that the homemade butter must be sweet and good. Too often homemade butter was not good and varied greatly in quality. That is one of the chief reasons why the consumption of butter has declined. Some of the homemade butter was like that referred to by the college student during his first semester away from home, when he said to his friend:

"The butter was so strong, it walked over to the cup of coffee and said, 'How do you do.'"

"Yes," answered his friend, "but the coffee was so weak it couldn't even answer!"

Speaking of coffee, how pleasant it was to come into the house on a cold morning after an hour or two of work doing the chores and find the house filled with the aroma of boiling coffee. But maybe that was the trouble. Coffee was *boiled* then so that, too often, it was bitter and strong and could be drunk only after plenty of cream and sufficient sugar had been poured and shoveled into the cup.

When I hear my friends, particularly young people, tell about skipping breakfast, I am sorry, for nutritionists are agreed that a good breakfast after the long night's fast is necessary in order to start the day's work. There was no nonsense about skipping breakfast in homes when I was young. After a hard two hour's work doing chores, it was good to face a big stack of buckwheat pancakes, well covered with butter and maybe maple syrup or molasses. But for some reason I could never figure out, Mother would never permit us to use syrup until after the first two or three pancakes had been eaten. Sometimes when she was out of syrup, Mother would melt some sugar for the pancakes. The first big stack didn't last long. I still have a vivid picture of Mother's face, red from standing over the smoking griddle, as she baked the pancakes which Father and we boys hogged down faster than she could bake them. The only rest Mother had from baking pancakes was during the hottest summer months, when we had to substitute bread or go hungry. If all the pancakes Mother baked in her lifetime were put end-to-end, I'll bet they would reach from Day Before Yesterday to tomorrow.

Of course, those old-time breakfasts did not end with the pancakes. There was a big dish of potatoes, fried or warmed up from the baked or boiled ones from supper the night before. The declining use of potatoes is another drastic change in our eating habits. None of the three meals Day Before Yesterday was ever complete without potatoes prepared in some form or other.

For breakfast, we had ham, bacon, or sausage in season. When those supplies were gone, we always had salt pork. All the pork products were grown and processed on the farm. Every winter there were barrels of pork in the cellar, preserved in brine and saltpetre. Fresh meat, except when we killed the hogs or beef, was rare and a treat.

The midday meal was called dinner, and I mean *dinner*. After you had worked five long hours in the field, there was no nonsense about lunch. Dinner was a substantial, cooked meal, with potatoes, meat, milk gravy, and pie. Almost always, we had milk gravy

for dinner and supper. I'll bet most of you don't know what I'm talking about. The gravy was made with milk, seasoned with salt and pepper, thickened with a little flour, and often made in the frying pan which had browned the salt pork. Makes me hungry just to write about it. Try it some time!

At night, for supper, we had meat again (usually salt pork), potatoes, and homemade bread. In season, for both dinner and supper, there were vegetables from the garden, especially sweet corn. Most people nowadays just don't know what sweet corn is like. To be really good, it must be picked just a few minutes before it is husked and popped into a kettle of boiling water before any of its delicious sweetness changes to starch. We used to have contests to see how many ears we could eat, as evidenced by the corn cobs we piled up by our plates.

At supper, Father and the rest of us never thought the meal was complete without sauce of some kind as a side-dish, not as a dessert. Since purchased fruit like peaches was expensive, most of the sauce came from the long rows of cans from Mother's cellar. Most of those cans were filled with wild strawberries, raspberries, blackberries, and cherries, together with vegetables canned from the home garden. One of the first things that a woman did when a lady guest came to visit in the fall or early winter, was to take her down to the cellar to point with great pride to the long rows of canned fruits and vegetables, most of which she had gathered herself and processed in her own kitchen.

One night, Belle's father and mother heard a loud crash in the cellar. Rushing down the stairs, they found a long shelf on which was stored most of the canned goods had given way, breaking most of the glass cans in a mess on the stone floor. You would have to have some experience with the hard work in assembling a food supply like that to know how tragic that accident was.

For supper, there was almost always milk and cake, but cake was usually just a single layer or loaf cake with seldom any frosting. For some unknown reason—probably because we boys got tired of it—we called it "soap cake," and the name still persists in our family. Also, probably because our soap cake was not particularly good, my younger brother and I got into the habit of crumbling it into a glass of milk and eating it that way with a spoon. That habit persists to this day, even with a three-layer frosted cake—when there is no company around! Some of my grandchildren have also acquired the habit of eating cake in milk. Try it.

I still eat lots of bread and milk, a habit I acquired when I was young. On the whole, though, children and adults of Day Before Yesterday did not use as much milk as they do now. Young people of today are milk drinkers and that's all to the good.

One food that must be included in any discussion of what our grandfathers used to eat is *corn*. Corn is and always has been king in America. It saved the Pilgrims from starvation, so it is natural that it should be used as food in many different forms. How many of you, I wonder, have ever eaten mush and milk, a standard Sunday night supper in the wintertime in thousands of rural homes. The mush was simply cornmeal, properly seasoned, boiled and dished warm into a bowl of milk. Any surplus was often fried and eaten, well buttered. It's good and it "sticks to your ribs." Corn was and is used in various forms throughout America—johnny-cake, corn bread, and corn pone. The flours of wheat and corn were not as refined as they are today, and for that reason they contained all of their natural vitamins and food elements which helped our ancestors to maintain health. It is also true that the longer a soil is cultivated, the more it loses some of its traces of minerals and other necessary food elements. So we supply those deficiencies now as well as we know how.

The "vittles" of our fathers were perhaps not as well balanced as they are today but they tasted better, particularly to the young, because the hard work of Day Before Yesterday made for prodigious appetites.

Because the farm cellar had such an important part in the food program of the people in years past, let's visit about it for a moment. Those old-time cellars were something wonderful. They were cool in summer and, because there was no central heating system, they kept vegetables and fruit well in winter. Occasionally, there was a night when the temperature outside was below zero, when Father would put two or three lanterns downstairs or keep a small oil stove burning. A regular late fall job was to haul straw or horse manure from the barn or barnyard, and bank the house with it all the way around, including the cellar windows, to keep the cellar warm. That banking made our cellar the darkest place on earth I have ever known. Without a light, you couldn't locate anything down there; even with a light, as a small boy, I never wanted to go into that cellar for fear something would grab me.

In the big cellar that I first knew, there were large and small pans filled with milk set to raise the cream. That homemade butter business, with all of its hand work, disappeared when we began to ship the cream to the butter factory or to the shipping station in our area. In the cellar were the hundreds of quart cans of fruit and vegetables already mentioned. Sometimes, 200 or 300 bushels of potatoes would be stored in the cellar, in the hope that the market for them would be better some time during the winter than it was when they were dug. What a tremendous job it was to carry all of those 60-pound bushels of potatoes down the outside cellarway in the fall and lug them out again when they were marketed in the winter.

Located in different parts of the cellar, in addition to the potatoes, were smaller bins or supplies of apples, squash (Remember those big green hubbard squash?

How good their yellow meat was!), onions, carrots, parsnips, turnips (white and rutabaga), and of course the big crocks of pickles.

What fun it was in the winter to bring up a pan of apples—Northern Spy, Baldwin, Greenings, or Sheep Nose. The trouble was, though, that Mother always insisted that we must sort out and use the apples that had started to decay before we could use the good ones. The result was that we were always eating rotten apples.

It was a big day in the late fall when Father or an older brother took a load of apples to the cider mill and came home later with two or three barrels of cider, which was used mostly for vinegar. I said "mostly" because we boys got outside of a lot of that cider before it got hard. I wonder how many of you old-timers ever took the bung out of one of those cider barrels in the cellar, just after the cider had started to work so that it had a little bite, and inserted a long straw or two or three of them into the delicious stuff and drank your fill of it. It tasted all the better if you could steal it, but you did have to be a little careful not to overdo it, or you would get a gosh-awful bellyache, followed by you know what!

Yes, we really used the cider that we didn't drink sweet for vinegar. But that was not the case with a neighbor who put 22 barrels of cider into his cellar every fall in order to make sure that he had enough hard cider to last until the next harvest.

Not only were those dark cellars dangerous to prowl around in without a light, but the stairs were often rickety and made more dangerous by various and sundry items which the women often stored on the cellar steps.

There's a story of the farmer who came in from the hayfield for his midday meal. His wife handed him a pitcher and told him to go down cellar and bring up a pitcher of milk. Stumbling over some obstacle near the top of the stairs, the man fell all the way down with only such interruption as each step afforded. Hearing the noise, the wife rushed to the cellar door and yelled,

"John, John, did you break my pitcher?"

"No," yelled John in a rage, "but, by God, I will!"

* * *

Well, the self-sufficient farms with their well-stocked cellars are gone. The modern farmer and his family are just about as much consumers as the city dwellers. Probably, if we could go back to the cellars and the "vittles" of former days, we would find that the cellars had lost their appeal and that the "vittles" are like the old gray mare—not what they used to be or what we thought they were. Maybe we would stop telling the wife what a good cook Mother used to be, too!

All the same, I would like, just for a week, to go back into that old farm home and into that cellar. Then sit at the table with my folks and my hearty boy's appetite. Or would I? I parted with my family once. That would be too hard to endure again. The next time I see them, I hope it will be forever!

* * *

Wednesday, Day Before Yesterday, was often the day for baking. Everything was baked at home, except one—that's me—who, my brother claimed, was only half-baked. Once a week, Mother made a big batch of bread, always starting it the night before. Standing at the kitchen table with long sleeves rolled up and flour up to her elbows and sometimes on the end of her nose, she pummelled and rolled that dough until one would think it would be black and blue all over.

Finally, getting the dough to suit her just right, Mother put it in several bread tins approximately four inches wide by eight inches long, and set them on a stand in a warm place back of the stove for the dough to rise. The next morning, that dough would be bloated up in those tins like the face of a boy who had been monkeying with a bees' nest. Then, with the old range going full blast so that the oven would be just at the right temperature to suit her, Mother shoved all those tins of dough into the big oven, completely filling it. Anytime in the next hour or two when a boy came into that kitchen, the aroma of that new bread would just about drive him crazy until he succeeded in getting some of it.

Then there were those homemade pies. Every mid-day meal had to be finished off with a slice of berry, pumpkin, apple, mince, or custard pie. Everything that went before was just an appetizer—a build-up for that piece of pie. The only trouble was there were six of us in the family, and when a pie was cut into six pieces, it was just not enough for the appetite of a hard-working farm boy.

Ever hear of apple grunt? When some pie dough was left over from the pie-making, Mother folded it over the apple pieces, sprinkled on some sugar and a little cinnamon, and baked it. Eaten with sugar and milk, one of those fat grunts could really make you grunt with complete satisfaction before you fell off your chair, dead to the world.

For a few days during the last of June, we often had wild strawberry shortcake. It was quite a job, picking and hulling those little berries, but nothing else I have ever eaten could be compared with that shortcake, made with one or two layers of baking powder biscuit dough (none of this cake stuff for me that you get in restaurants nowadays and is called shortcake). Over the biscuit were spread the berries and the juice. Then you took a big slice on your plate, poured milk or cream over it, and really went to town. If you have had the experience of eating a real wild strawberry shortcake, you will starve to death just reading this.

\* \* \*

The small modern kitchen, with its refrigerator, shining electric or gas range, running water (and other modern conveniences that my mother never dreamed of) saves women miles they used to walk in the big kitchens Day Before Yesterday. But what pleasant, busy places those old kitchens were, especially in August and September during the pickling and canning season. How vividly those of us who grew up around 1900 can remember the delicious odors of canning fruits and vegetables and all kinds of pickling. How many pickles can you name? There were piccalilli, mustard pickles, chow chow, sweet cucumber pickles, dill and bread-and-butter pickles, and pickled peaches and pears. How about that homemade catsup? Try and buy anything as good now.

Processed in those kitchens also were dried pumpkin, dried sweet corn, and dried apples. Some of you will remember the reason a hired man gave for quitting his job. He said the boss' wife gave him dried apples for breakfast, dried apples for dinner and let them swell for supper.

Yes, the modern kitchen saves steps and work, and I am all for it but, all the same, I'd like to step into one of those old, big kitchens in September, when the homemade processing is going full blast, smell the delicious aroma, and maybe get a big slice of newly-made pumpkin pie just like Ma used to make.

## CHAPTER SIXTEEN
# STORE CLOTHES-
# "HAND ME DOWNS"
# AND "SICH"

JUST THE DAY BEFORE I STARTED WRITING THIS, MY friend Harlo said to me, "With all the changes that have taken place in my life, there has been none greater than the clothes we wear, especially in what women wear."

"When I was young," he continued, "a woman could buy a pair of black cotton stockings for 10 or 15 cents, but it never made any difference what kind of stockings she wore because her skirts were so long a man never got to see them."

"If that was so," I added, "how did you know what women wore under those long skirts?"

"All hearsay," he retorted, "all hearsay."

But whether Harlo had first-hand knowledge or not, he was right about what women wore Day Before

How women dressed Day Before Yesterday. Look at those hats!

Yesterday and the changes that have come since. I had no sisters and no near neighbor girls when I was very young, so to me girls and women, except for Mother, were strange and mysterious critters. I don't think I was quite as ignorant on the subject as was one of my friends who told me that until he was a big boy, he actually believed women's legs were grown fast together above the knees.

I did know about women's hats because I could see them, and, believe me, they were something to behold. They were often made up from a good part of a flower garden and it used to be a source of great wonder to

139

me how women could stand the pain of running hatpins right through their scalps in order to hold their gorgeous top-heavy hats on.

Nowadays, women have changed their emphasis from hats to hair-dos; and some of the modern hair arrangements, where the strands come down irregularly around the head and particularly down on the forehead, remind me of an old sow we once had, whose hair reached down over her eyes so far she didn't know where she was going nor what to do when she got there.

Women of my boyhood, including my mother, combed their hair severely back from their foreheads and wound it in a tight bun back of their heads. Sometimes, when they didn't have enough of their own hair, they hid rat's nests in the buns. Now they're doing it again. Women took great pride—and rightly so—in their long, beautiful hair which sometimes fell clear to their waistlines or below.

When I see both men and women taking sunbaths nowadays, I often think how the women of my youth seemed so deadly afraid of sunshine. Except when they were working, they never ventured out in the sun without a parasol; and when I was very young,

working women all wore sunbonnets when out-of-doors. When these shadowed the faces of pretty girls or that of your mother, they framed the pictures we like to remember.

Old-timers will remember the shirtwaists with high collars. Once in a while, some of the bolder girls did wear "peek-a-boo" waists, which could intrigue the imagination. How in the world women of former generations managed to do their work in dust-catchers and floor mops, I'll never know.

Perhaps the greatest attraction of a good woman is the mystery of her womanhood, which is really the unsolved mystery of life itself. Why lose that great attraction by too much masculine clothing, or by too little clothing? Women would do well to leave more to the imagination, for it would be kinder to them than many of the sad facts that too much nakedness reveals!

Of course, I wouldn't know from personal observation, but I am told that the petticoats, corsets, and bustles that women used to wear were beyond the understanding of the men—and even of the women of today. I remember how puzzled I was when I was a boy and heard my mother scolding about a young

140

lady cousin who used a bedpost and pulled in her breath and held it so she could pull the strings of the corset so tight that she could hardly breathe. I was glad that *I* didn't have to wear any such contraption.

Hoop skirts were gone by the time I arrived on the scene, but pictures of them make me wonder how women ever negotiated them. With hoop skirts on, six women could fill a small room to capacity. It must have taken some skill just to sit down.

Ever struggle with a buttonhook, or with high-button shoes? Both men and women wore them. There was something to be said about high shoes, however, for they gave better support to feet and ankles than do the low ones.

Well, women tired of long dresses except for evening wear, and skirts began to fluctuate—or rather the hemlines did—like the stock market. They would go up and then down, but not so far down, thank goodness, as to drag on the floor, as they did in Mother's time. The reverse is true of evening gowns, since, as they go down at the bottom, they go down at the top—almost to the point of no return.

Lest I show any partiality, let's visit for a moment about what men wore Day Before Yesterday. Before the end of the last century, homespun clothes were a thing of the past. But I was a big boy before I got any mittens or socks from a store. Mother knitted them all, for the whole family. Until very recently, I had a pair of black mittens which Mother knitted so well that, with some darning, they lasted for half a lifetime. In my time, small boys wore waists that buttoned in front, short pants, and long stockings. It was a great day when I graduated to long pants. Today boys—and girls, too, for that matter—are almost born with long pants on.

When I was a boy, I got the hand-me-downs from my brothers. I was tall, so, like Washington Irving's Ichabod Crane, my arms hung from the too-short sleeves, and my pants didn't reach to the tops of my shoes.

You don't have to be too old to remember the celluloid collars and detached cuffs which were the last word for the well-dressed men. The celluloid collars could be cleaned with soap and a cloth and restored to their original shininess. Some of those old-time collars were so high that the wearer had to have a ladder to climb out of them to spit. Some of you will remember the fancy armbands which men wore above

Charlie and Fay, my two older brothers, all dressed up for church in the 1880's. Imagine trying to get today's children into all those clothes.

the elbows to keep their sleeves and cuffs from sliding down. Gaiters which buttoned around the ankles were the last word in affectation by the young dandies of my youth.

It was a big day in my life, when, in late fall, Mother took us boys to the shoestore and fitted us out with winter footgear. This included rubber boots, excellent for working in stables and any place where it was wet, but they were very cold in the snow on a winter day. Because they were airtight, rubber boots were never good for the feet.

The most comfortable wear for men and boys in the wintertime was felt boots. The felt came almost to the knees and over them rubbers would be worn that reached above the ankles. Wearing them, you could work all day in the cold and snow with warm feet. Some outdoor men still wore leather boots Day Before Yesterday, and when they became wet, as they often did, they would stiffen overnight. Then what a struggle it was to get them on the next morning, and it was even harder to get them off at night. I wonder how many of you would know what a bootjack was if you saw one. I have seen my father give up in despair, trying to get boots off with a bootjack. After

We bought our foot gear at the store Day Before Yesterday, but in Grandpa's time traveling cobblers made the family shoes, often from home-cured leather.

fighting the bootjack and losing, he used to hang onto the furniture while an older brother yanked and hauled to get his boots off.

Men who worked out-of-doors in the woods or on the farm always wore long woolen underclothes; that is, they were long until they had shrunk after being washed a couple of times in hot or warm water. Then you had to fight to get into them at all. By golly, how those woolens itched. Sometimes, when you got warmed up, you had to scratch so much, you hardly had time to do anything else!

What a relief it was when a boy or man could shed everything except a cotton shirt and overalls, except when he went to church or on a holiday. Then he had to put on those "store clothes." Those "Sunday go-to-meeting clothes" were enough to take all the fun out of even going to a funeral. It was good to get home from church or from a holiday and get into a shirt and overalls again. The relief almost made the Sunday clothes worthwhile—like the boy who pounded his head on the wall because it felt so good when he stopped.

In the summertime, we simply dropped our pants or overalls in the middle of the bedroom floor and jumped into the bed with our daytime shirt on. Like the modern hospital shirt, it was a little abbreviated but it served. In the wintertime, it was different. We had long woolen or outing nightdresses. I have never outgrown my liking for them.

When I remember the clothes that men and women wore when I was a boy, or when I look at the pictures of them, I can hardly believe the changes that have taken place from the formal dress, especially of the women of Day Before Yesterday, to the informality of today. Sixty years ago, no young man or women would be caught dead in public in the clothes young people wear now. The pendulum has swung too far to the extreme in dress.

One large high school I know of requires the girls to wear skirts, and the boys good pants, not sloppy jeans. The modern high-school building in which these students study is beautiful. Instead of objecting to the mild restrictions in dress, the students take pride in living up to their environment in both conduct and dress.

The perspective of time shows that there is not much point in the members of an older generation complaining that "things ain't what they used to be." Human nature being what it is, the pendulum will always be swinging from one extreme to the other and we can't do much about it.

My father and mother and their generation and those who immediately preceded them, reared in the Victorian age, were conservative in their dress. They insisted that no part of the human body, except for the hands and face, should be exposed. Now we have gone back the other way, but already there are signs that we have started to swing back again toward a more conservative dress. So there you are.

# CHAPTER SEVENTEEN

# READING WAS FUN

THE OTHER EVENING AT DINNER, WE WERE VISITING with a guest who grew up on a prairie farm in Dakota when that area was relatively new. I asked him, "What did you and your neighbors read when you were young?" He mentioned first *The Youth's Companion;* then a farm publication called *The Farmer,* which is still going strong in the Northwest; and a little rural publication called *Hearth and Home.* Among the books our friend mentioned, he put the Bible first, of course, then named others like Mark Twain's *Huckleberry Finn* and *Tom Sawyer,* the Horatio Alger books for boys and among school books, *McGuffey's Readers* led the list.

It was interesting to know that my friend's list of books and magazines in his western home as a boy was surprisingly similar to the reading material in our own farm home in the Northeast. In particular, I was interested to know that my friend grew up with *The Youth's Companion,* for I think that that weekly paper was more eagerly read and had more influence on young people of its day than any other publication. My brothers and I used to fight to see which one would get to read it first when it came, and Father and Mother read it as thoroughly as we did. One reason why each issue of *The Youth's Companion* was so eagerly awaited and read is the fact that there was so little to entertain rural boys and girls in those days as compared to the cars, record players, radios, and television of today.

Next to the editor, of *The Youth's Companion* Daniel Ford, the leading spirit and writer of that publication was C.A. Stephens, whose name became a household word in thousands of rural homes. Stephens wrote and the *Companion* published over 3,000 stories, all written painstakingly in longhand. Fearing that the readers would tire of so many stories written by one man, Stephens wrote under 40 different names. At one time, he had two continued stories in the *Companion* at the same time: one under the name of Henderson, and the other under his own name. There was considerable discussion in many homes, including mine, about who was the better writer—Henderson or Stephens. Imagine how both Stephens and Editor Ford must have laughed at the many letters they received expressing preference for one or the other authors!

I confess that as a boy I used to read dime novels—on the sly of course, for Mother emphatically disapproved. They were paper-covered sheets containing lurid stories of the exploits and adventures of heroes and villains engaged in murder and sudden death, entirely beyond the realm of fact. The *Nick Carter Stories* was one of these series. I used to hide my copies in the barn and under the mattress, for when Mother found a copy, she would burn it. I wonder what Mother would think about much of the modern stuff on the newsstands now. The dime novels of my youth were Sunday school literature compared to the reading material now available to young people.

Aside from the Bible, there are few books which have had as much influence in molding the lives of young people growing up Day Before Yesterday as the *McGuffey's Readers*. McGuffey was born in 1800. He became a teacher and educator, and in 1836 he was elected president of Cincinnati College. In that same year, the first two volumes in the series of Readers were published. The worth and popularity of these Readers (which finally covered every school grade) are proven by the fact that over 122 million copies were sold between 1836 and 1920. Not only the children but the entire family read them, and no one could read them without getting a fairly good knowledge of the classics and of literature in general. One has only to glance at the list of authors to be impressed with the selections to which young and old McGuffey readers were exposed.

To name a few, there were John Greenleaf Whittier, Charles Kingsley, Oliver Goldsmith, Leigh Hunt, Henry Wadsworth Longfellow, Nathaniel Hawthorne, William Cullen Bryant, Washington Irving, William Cowper, Daniel Webster, Amy Lowell, George Bancroft, Alfred Lord Tennyson, Thomas More, William M. Thackeray, William Shakespeare, Charles Lamb, Samuel Johnson, and many, many more. Do you wonder that *McGuffey's Readers* were a whole education in themselves?

When they were first published, rural papers and similar publications had no pictures in them; and I often wonder how our grandfathers, with their poorly-fitted glasses, managed to read the fine print. But the publications of those days had little or no competition. Even at the time when I was a boy, at the turn of this century, reading material was so scarce—at least in rural homes—that anything and everything was eagerly pounced upon and thoroughly read. Remember the stories of the difficulties Abraham Lincoln had to get something to read? His case was fairly typical of the scarcity of reading matter in his time and for many years afterwards.

The reading material in farm homes during the latter part of the last century and the first part of this century was not really complete without a copy of *The Old Farmers' Almanac*, which was really a small encyclopedia. Not only did it contain a calendar naming the days and weeks and months, but it was filled with recipes, hints on "how to do" on the farm and in the home, and all this was mixed with bits of homespun philosophy and humor.

I had to laugh when I saw, in one of these almanacs, a line written vertically in the margin that ran all the way up and down a page containing a three-month calendar. The line read, "along about this time, look for a change in the weather." The writer was taking no chances on being wrong!

Many farmers followed the *Almanac's* advice about planting and harvesting the crops, including planting them "in the moon." Personally, when I was farming, I preferred planting my crops *in the earth*. Yet, who knows for sure? The moon has tremendous influence on the tides. Maybe it has some on crops. And we do know for sure that the moon has great influence on lovers!

Although the number of magazines and papers that the farmers read from 50 to 100 years ago were very limited, almost every farm family subscribed to and read a farm paper. The Bible was well read. My father and one of my older brothers could quote long passages from the Bible, and from many of the classics. I don't know how many times I have read Daniel DeFoe's *Robinson Crusoe,* one of the greatest adventure stories ever written. Because our reading material was so scarce, we read and reread what little we had until it became a part of our lives. Many of the so-called "self-made men" owe some of their success to the fact that they got much of their education and wide knowledge through the reading of great literature when they were young.

In spite of the fact that the number and variety of books and magazines available today far exceeds the wildest dreams of people of my day, too many young people today have never learned the satisfaction and happiness that comes from good reading. Day Before Yesterday, there were no television sets, radios, automobiles, and social activities that take up so much of our time now. Still, anyone can find the time to read if he really wants to. One of the busiest executives I know reads two good books every week, besides keeping up with current events and the reading connected with his business. Think what reading those 100 books every year means to that man!

I like to remember those winter evenings when, with the chores done and supper eaten, the family gathered around the big reading table in the sitting room, lighted by the Rochester kerosene lamp with its green shade. Often there was a big pan of popcorn and a dish of apples. The round oak stove warmed the whole room and melted the frost on the windows. Every member of the family had a book or a paper, and there was a companionable silence as we relived with the authors the scenes and events of other days.

Except for the church and the school, nothing else has done as much to keep the community united and marching forward as the country newspaper. When a new school building was needed, or an improvement in the old one; when a library had to be established, a lecture course supported, water works or electric lights installed, the country weekly led the way. Frequently, it took plenty of courage on the part of the editor, for almost always progress faces opposition, and nowhere can that opposition be more personal, bitter, and violent than among neighbors in a small town.

Ever since I could read anything, I have always read the *Tioga County Herald,* the only country newspaper covering the three towns in Northern Tioga County (New York). In all that time, I can't remember a single project for the good of the community that the *Herald* has not supported. The same statement can be made, with truth, for most of the weekly newspapers throughout America.

Because of low income, all of the work of getting out the paper is done, more often than not, by one man—the publisher and editor. The result, generally, is that the publication is unattractive and hard to read. Yet it is safe to say that the country weeklies are better read and closer to their readers than any other publicity medium. Why?

The weekly newspaper is just about the last outpost of personal journalism. Nearly everybody in the community calls the editor by his first name and he in turn knows them all, their sins and their virtues; but he says little about their sins while he faithfully records their goings and comings and their personal achievements. Plenty of space is freely given in the local paper to the boy and girl, especially the girl when she marries—right down to the last ribbon she wears. Recorded always are the births of the children of that marriage, their achievements in school and college, and in life. When at last a native of the community comes to the end of the road, wherever he may be in the world, his friends who "knew him when" will learn of his passing in their old home-town newspaper.

Like many of these country weeklies and some similar city dailies, the *Tioga County Herald* publishes every week a column of news items taken from old issues. Because some of these little news stories are of historic value, full of human interest, and especially because my friend, the late Lloyd Allen—publisher and editor of the Herald—has used his grand sense of humor in selecting these old items, I give you some of them here with my comments.

*Nov. 18, 1891*

Last Friday night, the mail from Ketchumville, Lamb's Corners, and other eastern points failed to arrive on the stage and rumors of another great mail robbery were at once heard. A relief party was started the next morning and our citizens were relieved to find that there was no robbery, but the mail had been stalled because the horse hauling the stage had suddenly decided to quit the government service forever.

How young this country really is. That same stage route was in operation no longer ago than when Belle was teaching school and used to take the stage on Monday mornings from Newark Valley to her little school.

*Nov. 26, 1881*

Members of the Northern Tioga Agricultural Society will build a barn on the fairgrounds *if* they can get the money.

Apparently they got it, but the barn is now gone. So is the fairground. Time moves on but I still have memories of sitting in a democrat wagon near that barn at fair time when I was about 14 and holding hands with a girl. It was more fun than the fair itself, and that's saying a lot for a farm boy who didn't get a holiday very often.

P.S.: Another feller got *that* girl, but I got a better one and I kept her!

*Nov. 29, 1901*

While coming from school Friday, Harry Jayne, while running backwards, fell over a low wire fence, fracturing his collar bone.

Moral: Don't run backwards—physically, mentally, or morally.

*July, 1900*

Three different locomobiles passed through this village yesterday. One man had an experienced mechanic with him to keep the contraptions running. In a few years, these vehicles will probably become too common to attract attention.

I wonder what that editor would think now!

*Oct. 26, 1900*

Skunk-diggers were putting in good time Sunday on the farm of D. H. Andrews.

The lady who wrote those Anderson Hill items attained some fame as a column writer by expressing herself in spelling and language which were out of this world but so folksy and down-to-earth that just about everybody who read the paper read what she wrote.

Among her readers was the famous scientist, J. Alden Loring, of Owego, who accompanied former President Theodore Roosevelt on an exploring expedition in Africa. Loring thought so much of the *Tioga County Herald* and of the Anderson Hill items that he had the paper follow him to Africa. The result was that Teddy Roosevelt himself got to chuckling over the lady's column and read it every time.

Later, when Roosevelt came to Owego to see Loring, he said he would like to visit the author who wrote that marvelous Anderson Hill column, so the two very famous gentlemen drove to Anderson Hill. Pleased, but not in the least fussed with their visit, the lady got canned chicken out of her cellar and fed the men with the best home-cooked dinner they had had in many a day.

\* \* \*

*Sept. 16, 1910*

Will the man who took my hat at the Methodist Church please return it and get his old one back.

My, my—right in the church, too. What's the world coming to?

*Dec. 4, 1880*

The first ice of the season was cut back of the grist mill Saturday. The ice was seven inches thick.

Cutting the ice into blocks, hauling it to the ice-house where it was packed in tiers with sawdust, is another winter industry gone into limbo. It was not without its dangers, too, for sometimes a man would get a little too close to the ice's edge and get an icy bath.

*1910*

While at the fire Wednesday night, one of the firemen noticed a peculiar object in the shape of a horseshoe lying in the snow. Picking it up, he was astonished to find it was a set of false teeth. After having most of the men try the set on, he succeeded in locating its proper mouth in the face of a well-known merchant who, in his excitement, had never missed them.

Talk about cooperation!

*Nov. 24, 1911*

George Mix and helper shod 114 horses in four days in their shop.

No matter how busy George was, he always had time to visit with a boy and even show me some of the wonders of the blacksmith's trade, but there was handwriting on the wall for those old smithies. In 1911, the automobile was already on the roads.

*1900*

Work has begun on the enlargement of the Kemp factory.

It was in the foundry of that manure spreader manufactory that I earned part of my high-school expenses by helping to pour the white-hot liquid iron into the sand molds. I still carry a scar on my foot where some of the hot mixture spattered on me. When fellow workers cut my shoe off, there was a piece of cast iron, the size of a nickel, molded into my foot.

In one of those old-time foundries, with their dangerous white-hot metal, the shop filled with steam, and with the temperature ranging up to 100 degrees or more, a man was about as near hell on earth as anything I have ever experienced.

*Sept. 16, 1910*

George E. Smith, blacksmith, is making a new hose cart narrow enough to be used on the sidewalk. This will help the firemen to make better time getting to the fires.

Older people will remember that the worst roads in the whole county were often the village streets. They were a sea of mud after the rains, and inches deep in dust in a drought.

*Oct. 26, 1900*

The people of this town have paid out several hundred dollars this week for something like 30 different kinds of patent medicines. There is no habit which is more widespread or gets more of a hold on its victims than the patent medicine habit.

That good editor, long since dead, would turn over in his grave if he knew how people are eating and drinking patent medicines now.

*1910*

A couple of men went through town yesterday with eight half-grown swine. The only remarkable thing about this was that the pigs went straight through the streets. Generally, a hog is about as contrary-minded and as difficult to drive as a woman, but these pigs were led along by one of the men who had a pail of corn and he permitted his charges to shove their snouts into it occasionally. This man had the requirements of a good politician.

Right ! ! !

*1911*

Another year may see each battleship of our Navy having its own flying machine.

*That* was only 50 years ago!

*1900*

The first electric lights in town were turned on at the Kemp manure spreader factory last night.

That was long before electric street-lights were installed in the village. A familiar and nostalgic memory of my high-school days was the old lamp-lighter who traveled the whole length of the village with his bicycle to light the kerosene street-lamps in the twilight and retraced his journey in the morning to put them out.

*Jan. 7, 1882*

L. O. Eastman, school commissioner of Tioga County, informs us that he has moved his office from Owego to Berkshire.

The family has always been proud of my uncle mentioned in this old item. As a boy, he went to work early and got little education. Finally, in his 'teens, when he was working on a farm, Uncle Len decided to make something of himself and began studying. To make a long story short, he passed examinations for a teacher's license, later became school commissioner of the county, but kept studying all the time until he got through the medical college in Buffalo. After graduation, he became a very successful doctor in what is now Endicott—another success story made possible by hard work and the opportunities of this republic.

*Nov. 24, 1911*

One of the leading New York dailies recently printed its report of outgoing and incoming vessels on the same page with the obituaries. Somehow, the captions or titles were changed and a long list of respectable names were set forth under the Marine head: PASSED THROUGH HELL'S GATES TODAY.

Every editor has torn his hair over mistakes like this. Mark Twain (Samuel L. Clemens) used to tell the story about calling an editor on the telephone to expostulate about a news story report that Mark was dead. Mark concluded his criticism by asking the editor if he had any questions. "Yes, sir," answered the editor, "where are you calling from?"

153

# CHAPTER EIGHTEEN

# TAKE MY PILLS AND GROW FAT

**T**HE FIRST DOCTOR I CAN REMEMBER WAS MY UNCLE, who practiced medicine for more than half a century in the town where I was born. He helped me into the world. Maybe I shouldn't have been grateful for that, but, anyway, as soon as I got dressed, I shook hands with him, thanked him, and said "Good morning." He gave me a good morning in return and said, "Congratulations on a happy landing!"

Memory is a little hazy as to what happened for a few years after that, but I do remember walking along a dusty country road as a barefoot boy and meeting Uncle Dewitt, the doctor with the horse and buggy with which folks for miles around were familiar. Whenever Uncle saw me, he would stop his horse and say, "Hello, Eddie," and he'd give me a wink and a smile and then go on his endless rounds of easing pain.

As a small boy, I used to be invited once in a while to dinner with my Uncle Doc and my Aunt Kate, but all I can remember about it was seeing him carefully cut off a piece of steak, put it into his mouth, and then sit back with his arms on the arms of his chair and patiently chew that steak for a long time. Then, before the next bite, he would ask me how Pa's cows were doing. Oh yes, I do remember, too, thinking that I wished my Pa was a doctor so that we could have steak every day like Uncle Doc did.

But to this day it pleasures me to have some old-timer over in those hills tell how my uncle never failed to go on a sick call through the mud and dust of summer, and the snow and bitter cold of winter. The last day of his life he wrote a prescription for a patient who had come to his bedside for help.

\* \* \*

A neighbor boy with whom I grew up and with whom I roomed in school became a doctor. Roger Mead and I were chums from the time I was 12 until he died. When we were young, we shared everything, but Roger did most of the sharing because he was the soul of generosity and had more to share than I.

But no matter what Roger's obstacles or problems were, he never lost sight of his goal to become a doctor. And a doctor he became—and a good one!

One weekend years ago, Belle and I were visiting Dr. Roger and his equally interesting and likable wife and their boys at their summer place. In the middle of the night, Roger had to go out on a call. He was back at breakfast time, sleepless, tired and maybe a little discouraged. His wife asked him how the old lady was, whom he had traveled miles to see in the night. "Oh, coming along all right, I guess. The poor old fool would have got along just as well without me, and I could have had a little sleep."

Time and again I have heard physicians complain, particularly country doctors, that patients will wait all day with some kind of bellyache and then, just as soon as it begins to get dark, they get scared and call a doctor after he is tired from a long day's work. Maybe he had passed right by the patient's home some time during the day.

155

While he was waiting for his practice to grow, Roger used to come up to my uncle's farm, take off his coat, grab a pitchfork and help with the hay or with any other farm job. Once a farmer, always a farmer—with most of us who were raised on a farm. But when Roger was a boy, the neighbors used to say it was a good thing he was going to be a doctor for he couldn't even drive a team and a load through a gate without taking a post off on both sides.

Boy or man—Dr. Roger Mead was among the great.

\* \* \*

A physician who practiced Day Before Yesterday, Dr. William Gallagher was a man I didn't know personally, but I have heard my mother and her people tell so many stories about him that I feel as if I had known him. He galloped up to my uncle's farm home one time in the middle of the night, aroused him, and said without any preliminaries, "I want a horse." Uncle gave him one and put the doctor's horse in the stable with a blanket over him. When he went to the barn in the morning, the horse was dead—an incident among countless others showing how a country doctor let absolutely nothing interfere with

his getting to a patient fast and taking care of him to the best of his ability.

Living in Dr. Gallagher's bailiwick was one Sam Stone, whose wife, Sarah, was suddenly taken very ill. There were no country telephones then, so Sam walked and ran the seven miles to get Dr. Gallagher. When he arrived it was evening, and the doctor said to him, "Sam, it's been a long, hard day and I'm tired. If I come way out to see Sarah, I'll have to charge you two dollars." Sam hesitated for a moment and then replied, "I'll pay it, Doc, I've lived with Sarey a long time and I'm kinda 'tached to her."

\* \* \*

When my Uncle Dewitt (to whom I referred in the beginning of this chapter) died, he was succeeded in the same house and the same practice by Dr. Arthur Hartnagel, who married my cousin Katherine, one of Uncle Len's daughters. So for three-quarters of a century or more, Uncle Dewitt and Arthur Hartnagel have ridden the hills and the valleys of Northern Tioga County to heal and comfort the afflicted and help usher into this strange world many thousands of babies.

\* \* \*

Where the country doctor listened to most of the ills that beset mankind.

All of the kids loved Dr. Lockwood. There was a good reason why. When passing a group of children playing, he often would sit down in their midst, open his case, take out a bottle, and hand each child a little sugar pill. So he never had any trouble when one of his little patients was ill.

It was the same Dr. Lockwood who told the story about a friend of his who called him to examine his wife. After the examination, the doctor told the husband that his wife had a light case of tuberculosis. (They used to call it consumption.) And he told the husband that the wife must be taken to a warm climate. The man stared at the doctor for a moment and then, to cover his shock and grief with a grim joke, he left the room and came back shortly with a post maul which he handed to the doctor saying, "You do it, Doc, I can't."

\* \* \*

I could be wrong, but after living in country communities, villages, small cities, and New York City, it seems to me that there is much difference in the quality of medical service between the big cities and the small communities.

In New York, I had to conclude that many of the physicians seemed more interested in their financial returns than they were in the real welfare of their patients. And after considerable experience with doctors in *all* kinds of communities, I have to conclude that the modern doctors do not measure up in personal kindness and friendliness with the old country doctors. Those qualities are even more important in a doctor than his pills.

There are, of course, many exceptions to this statement. For more than 40 years, one of the best friends I have—as well as one of the best physicians I know—is Dr. Ernest R. Eaton of New York City and Brewster, New York. It has always seemed to me that Ernest could take one keen look at me and tell me what my trouble was without my saying a word. He is certainly the best diagnostician I have ever known.

One summer afternoon in 1932, I was fishing with Dr. Eaton on a little lake near Brewster, when suddenly we noticed that there was a strange, gradually deepening shadow over the land. In the woods on one shore of the lake, we could hear the sleepy twittering of the birds, exactly like they do when settling down for the night.

In a pasture on the other side, we saw a herd of cows starting for the barn even though it was only midafternoon. Then as we sat quietly with a strange, eerie feeling, it became dark. The bright sun was totally eclipsed.

Ernest and I seldom have met since without speaking of that eclipse, for it made an impression on us impossible to describe. No wonder the Indians were terrified when an eclipse occurred, believing that the Great Spirit had indeed turned against them!

One of the many reasons why I like Dr. Eaton as a physician is his complete frankness. He is always willing to tell you what he knows and thinks—and he is willing to acknowledge it when he doesn't know. Some modern doctors are learning that frankness is the best way to build confidence. Any intelligent person realizes that no doctor can know it all. One of Dr. Eaton's favorite sayings is: "Not all of the knowledge of medicine will die with the doctors."

The costs of modern medical and hospital service are particularly hard on people with modern incomes. Welfare takes care of the poor; the well-to-do can afford medicine; but the independent citizen who wants to pay his own way often fails to go to a doctor when he should, simply because he feels he cannot afford to.

One of my sons and his family have partly solved this problem by using the services of a cooperative group or organization which supplies both medical and dental services for an annual fee. But if middle-class people are to get adequate medical and hospital service, more must be done to put these within their financial reach. It seems to me that the leadership to bring this about rests with the health authorities and with the doctors themselves—not with the Government.

\* \* \*

When I was growing up on the farm, Mother always had handy a little tin box containing a white powder. Just the minute any of us boys began to get the sniffles or any other sign of a cold or grippe, out would come that little tin box and we would have to take a small pinch of that confounded white powder. It was quinine—and how I hated it, the bitterest stuff ever invented. But Mother was right; at least she had the support of generations of mothers in the use of quinine for colds and grippe.

The village pharmacist compounded many of his own pills. Compare this with the modern drug store.

When the settlers came into this or any other heavily wooded and swampy country, they were likely to get malaria, which they called by various names like swamp fever and ague, fever and ague, or Genesee fever. It was a miserable sickness. After an attack, you could think that you were well, and then it would start all over again.

\* \* \*

But Mother was not through with us after she got a dose of quinine down our throats, with its bitter taste that lasted for hours. She always had handy a bottle of castor oil. Now, if there is anything worse to take in the whole wide world than quinine, it is that awful stuff pressed from the castor bean. Whether Mother's remedies had anything to do with it or not, we got over our colds probably just as fast as we do now with some of the modern remedies.

All of you old-timers will remember without any effort other home remedies and medicines of our youth. All of them were characterized by a disagreeable taste that made some of them seem worse to a boy than the disease itself. Now as I list some of these medicines, you add to the list from your own experience. There was that standard springtime remedy of sulphur and molasses. Remember it? You will if you have ever taken it. It was supposed to "purify" your blood. Maybe it did, but my disposition wasn't very pure after I had been forced to take it.

Another standard home remedy along toward spring, after eating a heavy winter diet with few vegetables, was Epsom salts. This was given to relieve the almost certain indigestion which followed the heavy winter diet. On hand in many of the old-time homes, women kept a supply of Lydia E. Pinkham's vegetable compound as well as Dr. Pierce's golden medical discovery.

Ever take any skunk's oil, either externally or internally? If you haven't had experience with skunk's oil, you surely haven't "lived it up" for it was a common remedy when I was young, as it had been for many generations. It was given for colds or for an upset stomach, and by golly, the mere thought of the stuff now nearly upsets my stomach.

Then there were the many different kinds of medicinal teas made by boiling or extracting herbs like boneset, also used for an upset stomach.

Our mothers also were keen on poultices. There were poultices made out of pitch, commonly used on sores, as were those made from bread and milk. Then there were the plasters, like those made from mustard or wilted horse-radish leaves which were used as counter-irritants. And boy, they certainly could irritate if you left them on too long!

Were you ever told that you should eat the seeds of an apple as well as the apple itself? Apple seeds were supposed to be a blood remedy. If it was thought that you had any form of kidney disease, it was recommended that you should eat pumpkin seeds—shells and all.

Many of the old-fashioned home remedies came from the Indians, who believed—and they were partly right—that herbs, roots, and barks helped to prevent and cure disease. Some of the home-made remedies no doubt actually helped, if for no other reason than that they were taken with supreme faith. I had a famous doctor tell me once that he was certain faith had much to do with the efficacy of any remedy for our physical welfare as well as for our spiritual well-being. Certain it is that home-made medicines did not cost much. They probably didn't do any harm, and maybe sometimes did some good in times when doctors were hard to get and pay for.

\* \* \*

Dr. Arthur Hill was another friend of mine who practiced in the same village where I was a school principal. One time I came home from school for the noon meal and was suddenly taken violently ill. Belle did not want to leave me, so she sent five-year-old Don a little ways up the street to bring Dr. Hill. Not finding anyone in the outer office, Don barged right into the private office where the doctor was treating a patient. When the doctor tried to shoo the boy off, he would not budge, telling the doctor most emphatically, "Pa's awful sick. Come quick." In laughing about it afterwards, Dr. Hill said he understood how to obey an order, so he dropped everything and came on the run.

But I like to remember Dr. Hill as a flute player. He had lost his wife and must have been very lonely in his big house when day's work was done. I used to pause sometimes as I passed his house in the late evening to listen to him putting all his loneliness into the fine old ballads as he played them on his flute.

162

It was good to know that, before it was too late, the community showed their appreciation of Dr. Hill by recognizing and honoring him for his more than 50 years of devoted service.

\* \* \*

After we moved out of the town where I was born, Dr. Hiram Knapp became our family physician for many years. I am not sure how skillful Dr. Knapp was with his medicines; at least they were harmless, for he never handed me any pills without first taking one himself. But I do know that, better than all the medicines and the pills he carried, was his personal presence when he walked into a home where there was sickness. His never-failing cheerfulness and optimism had much to do with his patient's recovery. Dr. Knapp's faith in his own medicine, or at least his sense of humor, was reflected by a sign on his office wall which read, "Take my pills and grow fat."

As a small boy, how well I remember the black case that he and my Uncle Dewitt always carried that contained many bottles all in order and filled with so many different kinds of pills. I used to wonder how a doctor remembered which was which. How well I remember when I used to visit Uncle Dewitt's home the characteristic smell of drugs which pervaded the whole house, even to my uncle's clothing. That medicinal odor is gone now from doctors' offices and even from the modern drug stores, which, instead, have the delicate scent of perfumes, colognes, and talcum powders. Perhaps it is because I used to wish as a young man that I could become a doctor that the odor of medicine has a particular appeal for me.

For many years, Dr. Knapp kept my mother—who had a chronic heart ailment—alive and reasonably well and happy. I shall never forget seeing him gaze out the window of my mother's little home, with his shoulders shaking in deep grief, right after she had passed away.

*    *    *

In this modern age of specialization and greatly increased knowledge of medicine and surgery, it is too bad that the profession has become more impersonal and has lost that great quality the doctor of Day Before Yesterday had of making you his close personal friend as well as his patient.

# CHAPTER NINETEEN

# BEES
# THAT DID NOT STING

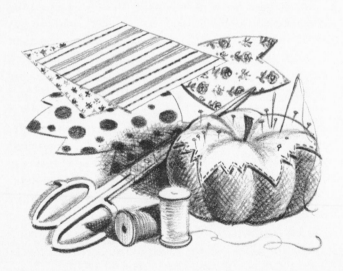

**I**T WAS A COLD, FROSTY DAY IN LATE FALL. FOR several days, Father and we boys had been busy moving the shocks of corn from the field to the big barn floor.

Our little black dog waited eagerly every time we tipped a shock of corn over to catch the big, fat rats who thought they had it made for the entire winter by living under the shelter of the cornshocks and eating the eared corn.

While we were working with the corn, Mother was busy in the house getting ready for a big feast for the neighbors who would come in the evening to help husk the corn, eat the food which Mother had provided, and drink quantities of sweet cider.

After the corn was husked, the barn floor was cleared, old Dan tuned up his fiddle, and the young folks danced in the light of the lanterns until midnight. If, during the husking, a girl was so lucky or unlucky, according to her point of view, as to find an ear of red corn, then she got kissed by most of the young men present. She always squealed a lot, but the squealing was for effect, for her resistance never was too strong.

That, with variations, was what an old-fashioned husking bee was like, common in most neighborhoods where corn was grown, from the time the colonies were founded until fairly recently, when machinery took over the husking job.

When I was a young boy, I was very frightened during a big windstorm to see and hear one of our old barns go down with a tremendous crash. This necessitated a new barn. After a couple of carpenters had worked a good part of the summer preparing the timbers and getting them properly laid out and fastened together with wooden pegs, the framework of the barn had to be raised. This required the help of many men, so, like in the husking bee, the neighbors all came over for the barn-raising bee. Equipped with long poles, and under the directions of the carpenters, the men raised the long timbers of the barn to form its framework and then finished joining them together. The job done, the men joined the women in the big feast the women had prepared.

*　*　*

On my bed there is a patchwork-quilt, containing 5,280 beautifully blended, colored pieces made by my mother toward the end of the last century. She kept it stored away in a big chest until I was married, then she gave it to me as a wedding present. The pieces are diamond-shaped, each one about one inch in size; and if laid end to end, the long way, they would reach 963 feet, or a little more than one-fifth of a mile. The quilt is still in excellent condition, and the design and colors outshine—in my opinion—anything else in my room or in any other room in which I have ever slept.

Seldom is there a day that I don't look at that quilt or others made by Mother's hands and think of the infinite patience and labor that she used in treasuring all the pieces of colored cloth, cutting them all very carefully to the same size so as not to waste any, and

165

My mother, Mrs. Elizabeth Eastman, when she was 79 years old, sitting in a rocking chair, 200 years old, with a quilt containing 5,476 pieces.

sewing them with beautiful, short, even stitches into that big quilt.

When Mother died, there were several big chests in her home filled with patchwork and appliquéd quilts. There were besides, the untold number she had given away during a long lifetime to her sons' families and to her friends.

In order to understand why so many thousands of women in past times, both in Europe and in America, made patchwork quilts, one has to know something of the barren lives that most of them lived. While my mother's life does not go back to Colonial times, she did live in the horse-and-buggy days before all of the inventions, the labor-saving devices, and the amusements of our modern times. Born in 1855, Mother was just old enough to begin her share of the household tasks when her father and oldest brother went away to the Civil War, leaving my grandmother to get along the best she could with a family of young children and a farm to operate.

As on most other farms, from the time of the first settlers to Mother's time, practically everything needed by the family, except for a few staple groceries, was grown and processed on the farm. From the time

An old-time barn raising bee. When the carpenters had the timbers all fitted on the ground, the neighbors came and with long poles raised them into place where they were pinned together.

she could do anything at all, Mother was taught to sew and sew well. Every scrap of cloth was precious, and when it could no longer be used to repair clothes, it was saved for the patchwork quilt. Until she died in 1937, Mother's chief pastime and amusement, other than growing flowers, was making patchwork quilts.

So far as recreation was concerned, there was little time or opportunity for most of the women of Mother's generation and those who preceded her to do anything but work.

Like millions of other women from Colonial times to this modern gasoline and electric age, Mother—and thousands like her—satisfied the urge to express their artistic talent by making patchwork quilts. It is amazing to know how beautiful many of the designs in the quilts were and how well the colors blended. Many were truly works of art. Varied indeed were the designs. The talent of the quilter was measured by the artistry of her design.

To me, the most appealing of all the patchwork quilts was the "memory quilt." Imagine how you would treasure it if you owned a quilt made with pieces of grandmother's and maybe great-grand-mother's wedding dresses and grandpa's wedding shirt,

167

with maybe some pieces from a dress of little Sally who died young!

The times of great national stress were reflected in historic, patriotic, or political quilts such as "Lincoln's Platform," or "Old Tippecanoe." One of the most common of the designs was the "star" quilt with an infinite variety of arrangements. Nature, of course, was well represented by designs of flowers, ferns, leaves, and birds. When the women made a quilt for the minister and his wife, it was natural to have a religious design. Think of the vivid colors in a quilt design called "Joseph's Coat."

The patchwork quilt had real utility value in the cold climate of the Northeast and the rest of northern America in the bitter cold, unheated bedrooms. It was heaven to sink into the folds of a deep feather bed and pull two or three warm patchwork quilts over you.

But more important even than the physical comfort of the patchwork quilt were the spiritual values. There is a true story of a great-grandmother of a friend of mine who migrated as a bride from Connecticut to a pioneer home in western New York. She was lonely and homesick during the first year of her wedded life. On the long wedding journey by oxteam from Con-

necticut to New York, she was comforted at night by the patchwork quilt that was spread over herself and her young husband. The quilt, made by her grandmother, seemed to bless her marriage. That quilt was with her when her babies were born, in the hours of sickness of her family or herself, and was always there during her entire lifetime, in bad times and good—a spiritual link between her old life as a girl and her new life as a wife and mother, an important link in the eternal flow of the generations.

Today, history has repeated itself and the patchwork quilts are back. You can buy them at the store, but they are machine-made and lack all sentimental value; they are not the same thing at all.

\* \* \*

When at last the hundreds or thousands of pieces were all sewn together, the quilt was laid aside to await the quilting bee. This indeed was a big event.

Up early in the morning, breakfast out of the way and the chores done, the women headed for the quilting party. The quilting frames were set up and supported on the backs of chairs. Over the frame was stretched the backing of silk or cotton. Fortunate indeed was the woman who could afford a silk quilt! On this backing was spread cotton batting or sometimes wool batting. Then the pieced quilt was laid over the top and the women gathered around all four edges of the frame to bind or tie the backing, the batting, and the quilt together, often with hundreds of little tufts of yarn.

The quilting was usually done in the parlor, which probably had not been open to the sunlight since the last quilting, wedding, or funeral in the family.

As they worked, the women traded food recipes and quilt designs and brought themselves up-to-date on the latest weddings and births, on those who were sick, and especially on the funerals. Many were the comments such as: "John looked so natural in his coffin that I thought he could almost speak to me"; or, "I wonder how long she will wait before marrying that hired man."

How well I remember one of those quilting bees, held at Mother's house when I was a small boy. Talk about "little jugs with big ears"! Will grownups never give credit to little boys and girls for what they know? Although I was apparently very busy playing in a corner of the room with a small brother, I still re-member some of the stories the women half whispered while tying off the quilt.

Come noon, the women took time off to empty the well-filled baskets they had brought from home. There was no dieting for them—in fact, I doubt if any of them had ever heard of weight reduction. I don't know how fair they were, but most of them who were over 40 were certainly fat. The meal over, they set to work again, finished off the quilt early in the afternoon, and all turned to prepare the big supper to which the men were invited. The men showed their appreciation by bringing appetites that always did justice to the great pans of baked beans, roast beef with gravy and vegetables, beautiful loaves of home-made bread, and all kinds of homemade relishes and jellies. All this was topped off by many kinds of three-layer cakes and delicious pies. Believe me, those men needed to do justice to every pie and cake if they were to continue in the good graces of every woman who baked one!

Back and forth across the long table weighted with about everything good to eat—nearly all of it home-grown and home-cooked—flew the kidding and joking of a happy, informal group having a good time.

When a man was sick, the neighbors made a bee and came to harvest his crops.

Then, finally, the big kitchen was cleared of furniture. Uncle Dan, the old fiddler, tuned up and they were off to an old-time country square dance, a fitting close to a long and happy day.

When the last of the guests had departed, the mother and maybe her daughters took the finished quilt off the frames, stowed the frames away in the garret until needed for another quilting bee. Perhaps the quilt went into a hope chest to await that sad yet glad day when daughter and young husband turned their backs on their New England homes to journey across the wilderness to make a new home beyond the western horizon. When they did, you could be sure the patchwork quilt would go with them,

Huskin' Bee! After the shocked corn was carried in from the field in the late fall, there was a huskin' bee usually followed by a dance and a big feed.

* * *

a constant reminder of the homes and the loved ones they would probably never see again.

Did you ever take part in a spell-down or a spelling bee? They were fun in town and country Day Before Yesterday. In a spell-down, the contestants, you will remember, stood up in a line and the teacher or someone else gave out the words in turn down the line. When you misspelled one, you had to sit down. The contest might last two hours or more before the last one in the line got caught on a hard unusual word.

In a spelling bee or match, each of two leaders chose an equal number of contestants who stood in lines facing each other. When one side missed a word, it went to the opposite side, and if spelled correctly, the one who missed it had to be seated. Excitement in the crowded, hot, smoky schoolroom, lighted by lanterns, often grew high as the contest got down to only two or three persons on each side.

\* \* \*

The many cooperative bees, some of which are described here, were an indication of the basic togetherness of the people of the neighborhoods Day Before Yesterday. Although our fathers were much more independent and individualistic than we are now, believing that they should not ask Government or anyone else to do the things that they should do for themselves, yet they knew that there were times and jobs when they had to have help. Those were the times when the neighbors rallied around in bees. They knew that no one walks alone.

They usually made a frolic out of their bees, with plenty to eat, and they asked nothing for their services except the understanding that if and when they themselves needed help, their neighbors would come on the run to render it. Uncountable are the times in village or country when sickness or death came to a neighbor, when friends came to take care of the cattle, to do the chores, harvest the crops, and even bring in food the family in trouble needed.

# CHAPTER TWENTY

# THE COUNTRY SCHOOL AND CHURCH

Still sits the school-house by the road,
A ragged beggar sleeping;
Around it still the sumachs grow
And blackberry-vines are creeping.

*Whittier*

MY FIRST DAY IN SCHOOL WAS NOT A HAPPY ONE! We lived on a high hill, three miles from the small village school, and I had to walk both ways. That was quite a task for a five-year-old boy but, somehow or other, I made it on that first day, got through the sessions, and was released early in the afternoon.

Grabbing my little tin dinner pail, I started on a run across the school ground to climb the hill and get home as fast as my short legs would carry me. I had not gone far on the school ground before a group of small girls, led by a larger, redheaded one, took after me and tried to kiss me. Under similar circumstances, I wouldn't run now, but then I had no sisters and no girl playmates, so girls seemed like strange little creatures to me and, like any other little wild animal, I was scared. I turned and bit the redheaded girl in the arm. I have sometimes wondered since then if doing a little more biting under such circumstances would not save us males from a lot of trouble! Anyway, the redheaded girl screamed, released me, and the next morning it took considerable persuasion on Mother's part to make me go to school again.

I often recall that experience on my first day in school, when I ride by the beautiful elementary school building which replaced the old one and which is named for me.

And I remember, too, the men who taught in those one-room schools which I attended. Once, in some strenuous play during recess, the entire seat of my threadbare pants gave way. Quickly noticing my grave predicament, the teacher grabbed me up in his arms, protected me from the unholy and gleeful gaze of my playmates, and took me down the road a-ways so I could get well started towards home and a good pair of pants. I was always grateful for that act of kindness.

Then there was Roy Barnes, the young, enthusiastic teacher who taught the next one-room school I attended. At the time, there were 10 or 12 out of the total of 40 or more pupils who were about my age and ready for high school. But few indeed were the farm boys and girls who went to high school Day Before Yesterday. It was too much of an undertaking, both financially and physically. We lived then five miles over the mountain from the village high school. If anyone went from our district or from any other rural district to high school at that time, his parents were doubly taxed. They paid their local school tax and also had to pay tuition to the high school. But Roy Barnes said that nothing was going to prevent any of us who wanted to from going on to get a high-school education, so he drilled us long and well. Then he insisted that we all should go over the mountain and take the preliminary examinations which would admit us to high school work. So most of our group did as he wished, and finally got the rather skimpy education which the high schools of those days afforded.

Because my parents were poor, in order to get the $40 for my tuition for one of my high-school years, I raised potatoes on shares with a neighbor. When the potatoes were sold in the fall, my share brought $40—just enough to pay my tuition. For safekeeping, I put the money in a state bank. The bank failed and I lost every cent. I had just started the year in high school and now I had no money with which to pay the tuition, so I went to Mr. Will Simmons, the local hardware merchant, and told him my trouble.

"Well, Eddie," he said, "I lost a lot of money too in that bank but we'll have to see what we can do."

Going to his old safe in the back of the store, Mr. Simmons took out four $10 bills and gave them to me. One of the greatest satisfactions in my life was the day I was able to pay back the $40. God bless the men and women who try to help young people who are trying to help themselves!

Another man in the same category as Roy Barnes was J.S. Kingsley, who, for many years, was principal of that village high school. No one will ever know, because he never talked about it, about the large number of boys and girls that Mr. Kingsley—like Roy Barnes and Will Simmons—helped on their way to an education and to a richer life.

I got off to a bad start with Mr. Kingsley. I had to help with the fall work, so high school was well started before I came over the hill to enter. I went first to the vice-principal who told me, bluntly, that I never could hope to catch up with the classes and that I must wait another year before entering high school and then must start on time. But I knew that it was "now or never," so I went to Mr. Kingsley's home and told him that I wanted to come to high school but that the vice-principal had told me I was too late.

"Of course you can come," said Mr. Kingsley. "Just wait here until I have had my breakfast and then we'll talk it over."

Now that seemed rather strange to me—that he should be eating breakfast so late; because I had been up early in the morning, had helped with the chores on the farm, had eaten my breakfast and walked over the hill—and he still had not eaten! So he went out into the dining room and left me

I taught in a one-room school like this Day Before Yesterday. I had no globe, though.

to wait. Nervous and scared, I sat down in a big easy chair and immediately got up again for I had sat on Mr. Kingsley's derby hat and it went off with a loud pop! I was greatly tempted to make a break for the door and forget all about high school, but I stayed. In a little while, Mr. Kingsley came back.

Pointing to the wreck of his derby, I told him how sorry I was. He laughed and told me not to worry, that he needed a new derby anyway. Right there was my first measure of the man.

After he had made me comfortable, he said that I could start in high school that very day and if I

176

had any trouble in making up the past work, he would help me with it. And he did. Not only did he help me with the high-school subjects, but I will never forget the inspiration of visiting with him in his study lined with books late at night. We visited about all the world with which he was so familiar, because he was so well educated. Years later, it was my privilege to become Mr. Kingsly's vice-principal in that same home high school. But when I first entered that high school as a student, Mr. Kingsley treated me—a green country boy—like a man. And he set my goals in life high and as long as he lived, helped me to keep them there.

\* \* \*

It was a hot afternoon in July. I was on my way with my oldest brother with the horse and buggy to see the trustee of the little one-room school that, years before, I had attended as a pupil. That memorable afternoon will always stand out in my mind because it was the last ride I ever took with my brother.

In spite of the fact that I would lack one month of being the legal age of 18 before my school year started in September, the trustee gave me the job—

the hardest one I have ever had. In describing that year as a teacher in that school, I can perhaps give you an idea of some of the aspects of educational opportunity—or, rather, lack of it—that prevailed in the schools (particularly the rural ones) at the turn of the century.

As a teacher, I was paid $30 a month for nine months. In the contract, which I still have, it was stipulated that I should build and maintain the fire in the big stove that warmed the little room and that I should do all of the janitor's work. The school had no library. It was difficult to write on the worn, warped blackboard. There were no screens on the windows, so the room was hot and filled with flies in the spring and fall; and no matter how hot the fire was when the blizzards howled, the room was cold. There were, as I remember, some 40 or 50 pupils of all ages, sizes, and temperaments.

I taught all eight grades, with subjects including reading, writing, spelling, arithmetic, geography, English grammar and composition, history, physiology and drawing. Most of these subjects were taught to every grade. There was therefore an almost endless succession of classes, with not enough time for adequate teaching of any class or any subject.

The one-room school in northern Richford within a few rods of where John D. Rockefeller, Sr., grandfather of Governor Nelson Rockefeller, was born. John D. moved away with his parents when he was a small boy.

The school was supported mostly by local taxes, which varied from one to thirty times among the different districts of the state, depending largely on the amount of taxable property in the district. Where there was a railroad or a large factory in the district, the tax was negligible. Where there wasn't, the tax was almost unbearable, even for the poor facilities which were provided.

Now we come to the teacher. We're always hearing old-timers tell about the great teachers they had in the little red schoolhouse when they were young. Memory deceives them! There were a few natural-born, excellent teachers in the one-room schools. Those are the ones remembered. But the majority were poor indeed. I had a high-school education far inferior in quality to that which high school graduates today get. In addition, I had a teacher's training class certificate, representing one year of professional training. I know that I was poorly trained, but I also know that my training was better than most for those times. Most of the teachers had what was known as a grade certificate, with no professional training. I know also that from the beginning of our school system in Colonial Days, teachers used the profession as a stepping-stone—as a way to earn a little money and gain a little experience—in order to go on to something that was more rewarding.

There were many incidents during my first years as a teacher in a one-room school that were enough to try a man's soul.

One time, I was playing ball with the boys during the noon recess. In stooping quickly to catch a ball, I completely busted through the seat of my pants. What to do then! I was miles from my boarding place and there was no time before the afternoon session to get a new pair of pants. I found an old overcoat that had hung in the cloakroom since winter. I put it on and taught school all afternoon on a boiling hot June day with that heavy coat on. Occasionally, I would catch a gleam in the eyes of some of the students but they didn't dare laugh too much. I have often wondered what the conversation was around the supper tables that night when the pupils told what had happened to their teacher.

When old-timers get together, incidents are recalled like the one where the older boys climbed onto the school roof and covered the chimney, so that when the teacher started the fire in the morning, the schoolroom immediately filled with smoke. Not knowing the cause, the teacher, to the great glee of the culprits, sometimes sent the children home.

All of us have heard or read the stories of how the older boys in the one-room schools raised Cain with a weak teacher in the many ways that boys knew so well how to do, until the teacher would have to resign. One can imagine how much education was acquired under such circumstances.

Some of you will recall, too, how the drinking water for the pupils had to be carried from a neighbor's home or pumped from a well in the schoolyard.

Over the pail or in it would be a small cup or dipper which served for all. I recall also the unsanitary conditions of those little houses out back.

Don't get me wrong. I have respect for some of the one-room schools and teachers, but the time came when they were not adequate for modern conditions any more than is the horse and buggy. There came a time when the country children had practically no educational opportunities compared to those who lived in the cities.

My teaching experience was enough to convince me that the school facilities in the state and nation were sadly in need of reorganization, for educational opportunity was far, far from what it should be. It is a wonder that the schools did as well as they did, but we were living in the horse-and-buggy times and perhaps the education we got, while of course not good enough, enabled us to get along fairly well in those times.

When the automobile came and the First World War was over, everything was speeded up and it became apparent that the educational system, based on the one-room school with only a comparatively few students going to high school, lagged far behind the needs of the people. So in New York State, the Committee of 21 was organized, consisting of representatives of the farm and educational organizations, the State Education Department, and the State College of Agriculture. After an intensive survey of school conditions in which hearings were held all over the state, the Committee of 21 came up with recommendations that the small, one-room districts be combined into large central districts, with equalization of the tax rate and greatly enlarged state aid.

The recommendations were accepted by the Governor and the state legislature in the mid-1920's. Then a campaign was begun, which has lasted over 30 years, and which has finally resulted in the centralization or consolidation of some 8,000 one-room schools in the state into about 500 central schools.

No one could ever estimate the tremendous increase in educational opportunity that this centralization has brought about!

Although methods of consolidation have been developed in the other states, the pattern of combining a large number of one-room, inadequate schools into central or consolidated ones is generally much the same throughout America. Not only have the cur-

h School teachers, Newark Valley, N.Y.
PUB. BY W.F. SAXTON

A high school faculty Day Before Yester-day. J. S. Kingsley, the man at the left, was the greatest teacher I have ever known.

riculums, the teachers, and the facilities been vastly improved for country children, but education throughout most parts of the nation, both in the city and the country, is marching on.

What a tremendous responsibility this great army of students is to all of us—the school authorities, the teachers, the parents, and, last but not least, the tax-payers. But we citizens of a republic *have* to accept this responsibility, for no democracy can long exist unless it is based on the right education of its people.

For some strange reason, it is only within the last 100 years or so that the right of women to an education has been recognized. But now, no one questions the right of women to the same educational opportunity that men have.

* * *

It is well for us to ask the question frequently: what is education, anyway? Why spend all the money and effort? What are we trying to do?

You will all have your own answers to these questions. I like to think that education is much more than teaching young people to be dollar-chasers. To be sure, it should help us to make a living, but it is far more important to know how to live. The world owes no one a living, but all of us owe much to others. Education should enable us better to serve our fellow man. No one has the right to travel the Road of Life without paying his passage, and education should help us to do it.

Another goal of education is to put us in closer touch with our environment. Two men can walk a country lane or ride through a lush farm country. To one, all Nature will talk; everything will have meaning. The other will see or understand little. It was William Cullen Bryant who said:

To him who in the love of Nature holds
Communion with her visible forms
She speaks a various language.

But it does little good for Nature to talk to us until we are educated to understand. Too many of us have:

Eyes to see and see not
Ears to hear and hear not.

Perhaps the most important goal or ideal of education is to increase our appreciation of God, of our fellow man, our country, and our marvelous inheritance. Tennyson said:

We are heirs of all the ages
Standing in the files of time.

That is more than ever true today. Old or young, our goal should be: *Teach us to see, O Lord, teach us to see.*

For many years now, the world has been full of wars and rumors of war, of armies on the march. I like to think of another army of nearly 50 million young people and their teachers marching, not to war, but to peace—marching to a new and better day for America and for all mankind.

182

In meeting houses like this one in Sturbridge, Massachusetts, the people of old New England fashioned a way of life that gave character and strength to a growing nation.

## THE COUNTRY CHURCH—ITS FUTURE

Years ago, when I was a county agricultural agent in a large county, I found myself late in the afternoon far from home, tired and discouraged. I happened to be passing a little rural church and decided to stop. Unlike most Protestant churches, which are kept locked on weekdays, this one was open, so I went in and sat for a long time all alone in one of the pews. It was peaceful and relaxing. The sun was shining through the stained-glass windows; no outside noise could be heard, and I soon fell to thinking of the generations of people of that rural community who had renewed their strength and their faith in that old church. I thought of the many young brides and bridegrooms who had stood before the pastor with joined hands and agreed to walk the Path of Life together; of the babies who had been brought to the church to be christened; and finally, of all the relatives and friends who had followed someone whom they had loved from the church to the little graveyard which adjoined it. After that quiet hour, I left the church with a sense of peace and inspiration which I will always remember. I don't think I was ever nearer to God.

My friend, Ed Thomson, pioneer leader in helping farmers to secure better credit facilities, once said that the Northeast is the land of cow barns and church steeples. It is certainly true that often, as you drive through the farm country, the first thing you will notice in many communities is the uplifting sight of a little white church, standing on a knoll, with its spire reaching toward the heavens.

The very first thing that the Pilgrims and the Puritans did after they had built their cabins, was to erect a church and school. All of us are familiar with the picture of the little church standing on a knoll, with the procession of Pilgrims in their ancient dress winding up the path toward the open door of the church. To build their church and to worship as they pleased was natural for the Pilgrims and the Puritans because they came here to secure religious freedom. It is strange, therefore, when they sacrificed so much to gain religious freedom for themselves, that they were so unwilling to grant it to anyone else. But then, the Puritans had no monopoly on religious intolerance. It is sad, is it not, that in religion, where we should most expect understanding and tolerance, there is so little of it?

Find what fault we will with the churches and with the hypocrites who are always to be found in them, and with the narrowness and the bigotry too often evident, the majority of the best citizens are churchgoers and try to live up to its high standards. All humans need standards of conduct, and entirely aside from what may happen to our souls when we are done here, we need the associations of our fellows and the help of God to be clean and decent and good.

In his book, *Empty Churches,* Charles Josiah Galpin said, "Narrow and bigoted as the religion of our fathers no doubt was, yet its teachings of responsibility and of the love of God and man were so interwoven into the characters of the country boys and girls that the most of them carried those principles throughout their lives."

But while we like to think of Ed Thomson's statement about the land of church steeples, unfortunately it is only an ideal, for it is not true of every community. It is true also that the progress of true religion in America has been sadly handicapped in thousands of communities by too many churches rather than too few, with the result that there are neither members nor finances enough in any of the several churches of the community to pay a competent minister or support other needed church activities.

In the strictly country community where I spent most of my boyhood, there were four churches within a five-mile radius. There was not a big enough attendance at any one of the churches to justify a full-time minister. Over the hill to the east in the next valley, in a small country village of less than 1,000 inhabitants, there were four churches and an equal number in another village over the hill to the west.

Concerning the country church in 1927, I said: "This is the age of cooperation, of coordination, and of consolidation, yet the churches have been slow to see this, slow to get together. There are thousands of communities in strictly farm sections and in small villages where two, three, or four churches now starving along with a poorly trained and underpaid minister and an overtaxed congregation could unite, hire a well-trained man and insure him adequate financial and spiritual support from a large congregation. That must be the first step in any adequate program of bringing back religious training to country districts."

But it is good to be able to report that able efforts are being made in every state to bring the rural church up to its wonderful possibilities. In New York State, the Rural Church Institute, now directed by Stanley E. Skinner, is making real progress in dozens of communities in helping local leadership to bring several churches of a community together, working with several different kinds of plans.

In a recent statement, Reverend Skinner said, "Certainly one of the most significant aspects of present-day religious life in America is that, in spite of the number of our denominational traditions, we are discovering a unity that extends beyond our denominational fences."

I might add that we Americans are impatient people. We expect too much in too short a time. It took nearly a half-century to consolidate the schools in one state and they are not all consolidated yet in the nation. So perhaps we should be encouraged that, as Mr. Skinner says, denominational fences are breaking down. For ". . . the mills of God grind slowly . . ."— but grind they do.

# CHAPTER TWENTY-ONE

# WHERE <u>NOW</u> SHALL WE LOAF AND LIE?

### *THE COUNTRY STORE*

WHEN I WAS ABOUT FIVE YEARS OLD, I HIRED OUT TO my father to work for him for a month for $30, and I was to pay him $29 a month for my board and room. At the end of the month, which came near Christmas time, he kept his agreement and gave me a big silver dollar, the first money I ever earned.

I wish now that I had kept that dollar. On second thought, I guess I would rather have the memories of how I spent it. I went with Mother to the village to buy Christmas presents with that dollar for my family. It had to be enough to buy a present for Father and Mother and my three brothers, and I made it do. I cannot remember the presents I bought but I know it was the best dollar I ever have spent for anything.

The chief reason why the dollar was sufficient was the good suggestions I got from Mother and especially from Mr. Eddie Eldridge, the storekeeper. That old country store was a fairyland, and the kindly merchant who owned it was a prince to a small boy. I never went into that store without his giving me a long penny stick of striped candy or some licorice which I hoarded and made last for days.

It is said that the sense of smell is more closely connected with memory than any of our other senses. I believe it. I can close my eyes today and bring back vividly the delicious and interesting smells of Mr. Eldridge's store.

Usually, Mother bought the coffee in the bean, and ground it in the small hand coffee mill at home every morning before breakfast. But sometimes she got Mr. Eldridge to grind it in his big coffee mill in the store. That delicious smell in our house before breakfast and the smell of the coffee in the store, when Mr. Eldridge ground it in his mill, would whet anyone's appetite. Maybe Mr. Eldridge's store smelled so nice because it had a combination of smells, as did all the old-time country stores. The odors seemed to fit together to intrigue and remain in a boy's memory.

I'll bet you old-timers remember that big cylindrical cheese, with its glass cover, which always was on the store counter. Nearby was the cracker barrel, and it was always sort of taken for granted that you could help yourself to a handful of crackers as you went by the barrel. Has any meal ever tasted better to you than those times when you drove a load of produce to market, maybe on a cold, fall day, then went into the little store for your noonday lunch to eat your fill of the delicious cheese with all the crackers you could hold? Perhaps as you sat on a stool by the counter while you were eating, you had time and big ears to listen to the loafers who sat in armchairs, provided by the merchant, around the glowing coal stove as they argued and told stories. Sometimes you gazed in wonder at some old bewhiskered citizen who spat tobacco juice at a distant spittoon with an accuracy that would have done credit to a sharpshooter.

\* \* \*

Nowadays, every housewife talks about *shopping* for her groceries or other supplies. But in the horse-and-buggy times, the word was "trade." Often it meant literally that—trading farm supplies, chiefly eggs and butter, for the groceries.

Boy or man, the country store was the most fascinating place in town. How many items can you name?

Just recently, someone wrote me a story (which my friend said was true) of an old-time grocery store. A woman entered the store with a package of butter. She said quietly to the merchant, "I have some butter here that I would like to trade for some of yours. Frankly, a rat fell into the cream so no one of my family will eat the butter, but I thought you could trade it for yours and no one will ever know the difference. What they don't know won't hurt them any." The merchant took her butter and went to the rear room, but instead of exchanging it for some of his own, he rewrapped hers, returned it to the woman, telling her, "What people don't know won't hurt them any."

On the subject of the country store, a letter I received today from a friend reads as follows:

Although I lived in the country until I was 15 years old, my father wasn't a farmer. He operated a country grocery store. The store was lighted with old-time kerosene lamps and it was open from 7 A.M. to 10 P.M. or later, if the checker games of the loafers were not over by 10.

Another Vermont farmer wrote me some time ago about playing checkers, when he was young, with an older friend in the back room of his friend's country store. While they were playing, the front door of the store opened, which made a little bell jingle, but the storekeeper paid no attention. Finally, my friend reminded him that there was a customer out front. "Yeah," said the storekeeper, "keep still and maybe he'll go away."

I had an uncle who, when day's work was done, frequently drifted to the village store to swap gossip and lies with the other "setters" around the big stove. He used to tell a story about a stingy old fellow who wore a pair of overalls which were so stiff with dirt that they could almost stand up by themselves. One evening, the old fellow came into the store to make a small purchase. Making sure that there were no women around, the other men locked the store door, grabbed the old man, and stripped him of his dirty old overalls. Then, pulling a new pair from the shelf, they put them on him, took his pocketbook from the old pair, carefully opened it so that the storekeeper could see just what they took from it, and paid for the new pair of overalls. Far from being mad, the man mumbled something like: "Should have done that a long time ago m'self." Then he marched proudly out of the store in his new "bib 'n' tucker."

The crossroads country store at Caroline Center, New York in 1910—a pleasant place to loaf.

Well, like so many of the customs and the doings of Day Before Yesterday, the country store has mostly gone from the American scene, replaced now by the "serve-yourself" chain stores and the supermarkets with all of their high efficiency and spotless sanitary conditions. I wouldn't want to change them but, just the same, it would be fun again to go with my uncle into the village store that we knew long ago, typical of thousands across the country, listen to the arguments and kidding of the "setters," and smell the conglomeration of tobacco, smoky oil lights, coffee, cheese, and so on that we will never smell again. At the same time, I'd like to be a boy again and watch the old merchant (at least he seemed old to me at the time) measure off from the bolt of calico with unerring accuracy the yards of material for milady's dress. It would be fun, too, to watch with other kibitzers a couple of old-timers play a game of checkers on a checkerboard marked off on wrapping paper, with peppermint and wintergreen lozenges for checkers, when occasionally one of the players would absent-mindedly forget and slip one of his opponent's captured men into his mouth!

## THE BARBERSHOP

Closely allied with the village blacksmith shop—so far as loafing was concerned—was the barbershop. There seldom was more than one barbershop in a small village. The barber knew every man in the village, many of the farmers around, and they all knew him. In fact, how could he forget them? Not only did he cut their long and woolly hair, but once a week, usually on Saturday, he shaved them—or at least those who did not sport a beard or a handle-bar mustache. Then there were those shaving mugs. On a shelf against the wall of the shop, there was always a large, shallow, open cupboard, divided into spaces just large enough to hold a shaving mug on which was printed the owner's name. Some of the owners, frustrated in any other way of expressing their personalities, took that frustration out on those decorated mugs with their names on them.

When you climbed into the barber chair, you had to fortify yourself against the barrage of words that filled the air from the "sitters" around the room awaiting their turn, and from the loafers who were always there, whether they needed the services of the barber or not. But the barber was an old hand at that business. He should be, for he had lots of practice. The hours that the old-time barbers served were ghastly. No wonder they talked! The barber opened his shop and his mouth at 7:00 in the morning, and stood on his feet until 6:00 or later every night. On Saturday, his biggest day, he did well if he got to bed by 11:00. For his service, he collected the magnificent sum of 25 cents for a haircut and 10 cents for a shave.

One barbershop that I once knew was the headquarters of the local "Spit and Whittle Club." When a man retired from work, or just got tired of it, he joined the group. In winter and in stormy weather, the members lined the walls inside the barbershop. In summer, they tipped their chairs back against the walls on the outside. Sometimes the members sat quietly, meditating perhaps on their sins. Sometimes when they were outside the shop, they watched the girls go by, thinking sadly of their own lost youth. But inside or out, the discussions and the debates on all and sundry subjects often waxed hot and furious. The subjects ranged from the length of women's skirts, the scandalous conduct of some local female, how the young people were going to damnation on a handsled, to politics and religion.

One barber in the village near where my uncle lived was deeply religious, so he never would permit the highly flavored stories that often enlivened barbershop conversation. When talk got off from religion, the barber would slow down his work, but when he could get it back on hell-fire and damnation subjects, then he could shear the long locks off at lightning speed, or shave you in no time flat, without a single nick.

As a boy, getting one's hair cut, even for 25 cents, was a real luxury. What a treat it was to have a really good job done by the barber with that sweet-smelling stuff which he put on your hair afterward that made you smell so good for the rest of the day! Most of the time, Mother cut my hair. She had many great virtues, God rest her soul, but hair-cutting was not one of them. After she finished working on me, an older brother used to call me "baldy-head" or "peeled-head." The insult was based on the fact that Mother didn't believe in cutting hair often; so with her dull shears, she got all of it off that she could, leaving bare spots in places. How I hated it and the hairs that got down my neck and itched and itched until I got a bath a month or so later.

There was another thing about those old barbershops that I miss now. They were one of man's last retreats. A female would rather have been caught dead than be seen in one. But now, the gals have taken over the barbershop—along with our pants, our smoking tobacco, and our liquor. I'd say it's time for us men to rebel.

## THE VILLAGE BLACKSMITH SHOP

After a long, hot, dry spell filled with days of hard farm work, how welcome a rainy day was to the hired man and to us boys! How disappointed and disgusted we were when it was cloudy in the morning, with every promise of rain, only to have it clear up so we would have to work in the fields after all. "All signs fail in a drought."

One of the chores on a rainy day was to take the team of horses to the village blacksmith shop to get them shod. That was fun. The old-time blacksmith shop had a peculiar smell all its own—a mixture of smoke from the charcoal burning in the forge, of hot iron, and burning horses' hooves. Almost always, on rainy days, there were several horses waiting their turn to be shod, while their owners—the men and boys—plus the ever-present village loafers sat around, told stories, and watched the hard-working blacksmith blow his little fire in the forge to bring the metal almost to a white heat. It was fascinating to see the smithy pick the hot shoe from the forge with his long forceps and pound it on the anvil until he got it just the right shape. I can still hear that anvil ring. Before fitting the shoe, the smith picked up each foot of the horse and held it between his legs while he trimmed the foot. Then, as he pounded the shoe into shape, he tried it from time to time on the horse's foot to make sure that it fit before he nailed it fast.

As we waited, we traded the news and the gossip accumulated since the last time we had brought the horses to the shop. We boys added materially to our education on the facts of life, mostly false, from the conversations of the older men. Some of the old chestnuts told and retold in one form or another since the days of the Founding Fathers were really funny, even if you had heard them 16 times before, especially when they were applied to someone who was present or to some character in the neighborhood whom everybody knew. For example, there was the story told about the local hired man whose first name was John, who sometimes came out second-best in his fight with John Barleycorn. John, it was claimed, was hurrying one Saturday night from the farm where he worked to the village when he met a neighbor who asked him where he was going. John said, sourly, "Goin' to town to git drunk—an' God, how I hate it!"

The skill with which most blacksmiths could handle all horses, including the mean ones, was uncanny. I knew and could drive all kinds of horses, including the balkers and the kickers, but I drew the line at picking up the hind feet of a mean one. Not so with the blacksmith. The ones I knew never hesitated. One of them used to carry sugar cubes in his pocket

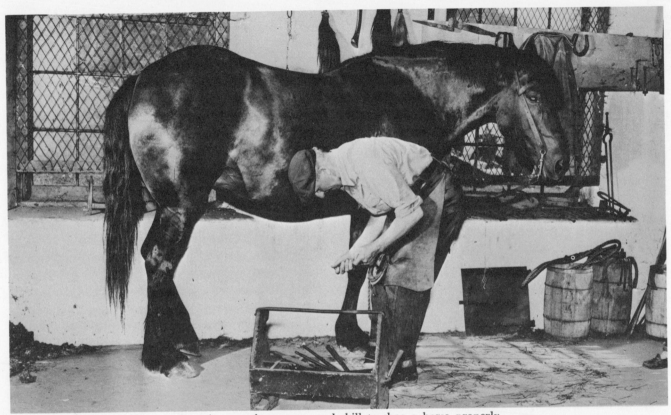

It took strength, courage, and skill to shoe a horse properly.

and, after petting a mean horse and talking to him very gently for a moment and feeding him a little sugar, the smith could do anything with the horse that he wanted to. It was the irony of fate that when a blacksmith I knew retired from his trade to farm, he was kicked in the head and killed by one of his own horses.

One day a farmer brought a horse to the shop of the village blacksmith, warned the smithy that the horse was dangerous and that he, the owner, would have to be present when the blacksmith shod him, for the horse would probably have to be roped and thrown before he could be shod. The smith said, "All right, Joe. There are some others ahead of you, so go on and do your errands and we'll shoe your horse when you get back." As soon as the owner was gone, the smith began talking to the man's horse, and in a few minutes had taken off the old shoes, trimmed up the hooves, and put on the new shoes, all in the usual way, while the horse made no trouble at all. Can't you imagine how astonished the owner was when he got back?

In its day, blacksmithing was a highly skilled trade, but now it has gone into limbo, like so many skills and trades of Day Before Yesterday. But not gone with some of us are the memories of the cheerful laughing, singing, and whistling of the smith himself while he pounded his ringing anvil, which will sound no more.

Longfellow described the village blacksmith well when he wrote:

Toiling,—rejoicing,—sorrowing,
Onward through life he goes;
Each morning sees some task begun,
Each evening sees it close;
Something attempted, something done,
Has earned a night's repose.

# CHAPTER TWENTY-TWO

# VENDUE
# "GOING-GOING-SOLD TO-"

IN 1943, WHEN BELLE AND I BOUGHT THE FARM ON Route 13 near Etna, Mrs. Mabel Rhodes, the former owner, held an auction to sell off some of the furniture and farm tools which she did not have room for in her new place. Before the sale started, Belle and I saw a big empty pork barrel in the cellar and we both decided we would buy it. But when the auction started, there was the usual big crowd and Belle and I became separated. So when the pork barrel was put up for sale, we both started to bid on it. The auctioneer, Frank Taylor of Cortland, knew us both, but instead of stopping us, he thought it was a huge joke and he let us go on bidding against each other. So each of us kept on getting madder all the time, and bidding the price of the barrel well over its actual cost because we were determined that, come hell or high water, we were going to have that barrel!

My friend, the late Carl E. Ladd, dean of the New York State College of Agriculture, stood right beside Belle while she was bidding, and, from where he stood, he could see that I was the one bidding against her. I never saw anyone laugh more than Carl did over this, and afterwards he never failed to ask me how the pork barrel was doing.

The other day I went over to call on Mr. Taylor and I told him he ought to be ashamed of himself because he had broken up a happy home, for Belle and I had never spoken to each other since!

\* \* \*

After we had that settled, I got Frank busy telling stories about the funny things that have happened at auctions. Incidentally, Frank Taylor has the well-earned reputation of being one of the best auctioneers in central New York.

I have been going to auctions all of my life, for I know of no other place where one can see so much human nature in action. It would take a book to tell you some of the things I have observed and especially some of the stories that Frank told us the other day about his 20 years of experience in crying auctions.

I asked Frank if—had he his life to relive—he would be an auctioneer. His answer was indicative of the kind of man he is. He said, "Yes, I would be either an auctioneer or a minister." Then he went on to give us some of his philosophy.

"To be a good auctioneer," he said, "you have to have control of the crowd and their interest all of the time. You have to use both philosophy and humor. An auctioneer must not only understand people, he must know the market values of the individual articles he is selling, and he must have a psychic sense to know just when to let the article go."

I might add that an auctioneer must also have the voice and the endurance of a giant. Frank uses a tent and a microphone now, but he really doesn't need the "mike."

"There are different kinds of auctioneers," Frank continued, "the crabby, sourpuss kind, and the wise guy who knows it all and forces himself on the crowd. The old-time auctioneer who strutted around with a

# AUCTION

The Subscriber will sell at Public Sale at his residence

## 1-2 MILE SOUTH OF FIVE CORNERS on

# Wednesday, March 11, '14

Commencing at 12 o'clock sharp, the following property:

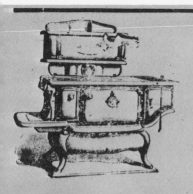

Top buggy, democrat wagon with top, cutter, 2 sets single harnesses, fly nets, 2 inch basswood lumber for rigging, a lot of sawed wagon tongues, lawn mower, lawn swing, hot bed sash, creamer, barrel churn, milk separator, ice cream freezer, counter scales, 10 casks vinegar, quantity carpenter tools, tool chest.

## HOUSEHOLD GOODS

Extension tables, 4 drop leaf tables, couch, hair cloth sofa, 2 bureaus, bedsteads, 4 feather beds and pillows, 75 yds. carpet, cupboard, sitting room and dining chairs, several easy rockers, stands, mirrors, pictures, 4 clocks, gasoline lamp, writing desk, caron board, book case, iron sink, jugs and jars, Andes range, cook stove, chunk stove, washing machine and tubs, a full line of dishes, tinware, glassware, lamps, knives and forks, spoons, etc., 2 20-gallon pork jars, about 50 lbs. salt pork and many articles not mentioned.

*TERMS*-All sums of $10 and under cash; over that amount a credit of 9 months will be given on good approved, endorsed, interest-bearing notes, payable at the First National Bank of Genoa.    No goods removed until settled for.

J. A. Greenfield, Auctioneer,
Claude Palmer, Clerk.

# FRANK CORWIN.

TRIBUNE PRINT, Genoa, N. Y.

cud of tobacco in his mouth, his white vest stained with tobacco juice, will no longer get across.

"There are three kinds of auctions: One, the auctioneer works on a commission basis; two, he works for a specified sum of money (bid crier); and three, the auctioneer works for an auction house.

"Among those who attend auctions," Frank said, "there is the person who wants to bid but hesitates to get started, others who do not wish to be made conspicuous by having their names called out, and dealers who do not want to be recognized, since they plan to resell the articles."

Frank also said that, once in a while, someone will bid up an article just to prevent some other person whom he does not like from getting it, or in order to make that person pay a high price. There are people who go to auctions frequently just for the entertainment of it. He told of an elderly lady who broke her hip. She telephoned Frank to say that she didn't mind the broken hip so much as she minded its preventing her from attending his auctions.

Some people have a disease which might be called "auctionitis." They attend every auction they can get to, bid on almost everything whether they need it or not, with the result that their homes and premises finally become so filled with trash that you need a guide to get around in them.

I asked Frank if there is any difference in bidding between men and women. "Yes," he said, "women are not consistent bidders. They will bid for awhile, stop, and later start bidding again. And as a rule, women are a little more likely to get mad or emotional when somebody is bidding against them. Then they'll bid higher than the article is worth. There are exceptions, though."

I discussed with Frank a good rule about knowing when to stop bidding. He agreed with me that when buying a second-hand article, one shouldn't pay over half the retail price of a new one. Frank feels that an auction is an ideal place for a young couple to get things for their new home.

\* \* \*

I have before me a large, old-time auction bill which Frank loaned me. It is dated March 11, 1914. Pictured on it is a kitchen range with reservoir and overhead warming oven. On the opposite side of the poster is a picture of a buggy. The items mentioned for sale indicate the tremendous change that has taken place in our way of life in the last half-century. To mention a few items from the bill, there are: hair cloth sofa, swell-body cutter, harnesses, fly-nets, churn, feather beds, kerosene lamps, chunk stoves, and so on.

It was a curious coincidence that Frank conducted an auction on this same farm more than 40 years after that first sale.

Frank told us that sometimes, when the bidding slows down and he can't get the right price, he just rolls his tongue without saying anything in a manner impossible for me to imitate, but perhaps you can get the idea from the following:

Ah-l-bl-blah-bl-bl-blah-Ah-bl-bl-blah-bl-bl-blah

Ah-l-l-la-l-l-la-Ah-l-l-la-la-la (continue rolling the tongue)

When we were ready to leave, I handed Frank an old everyday hat that I have had around at least 10 years and asked him to sell it. He hesitated for a moment, a little embarrassed, because he said he lacked the inspiration of a large crowd. Then he got started and, after a few words, he was in full swing. Here's what he said, talking faster and faster as he neared the climax. When he came to the word

"whoops," you could have heard him for a mile.
"Now, here's a fine Stetson hat
Light gray, good condition
A little worn around the edges
Lot of good in it yet—
"I've-got-a-quarter, who'll-give-me-a-half?
I've-got-a-quarter, who'll-give-me-a-half?
I've-got-a-half, who'll-give-me-seventy-five?
I've-got-a-half, who'll-give-me-seventy-five?
Whoops! I've-got-seventy-five, who'll-give-me-a-dollar?
I've-got-seventy-five, who'll-give-me-a-dollar?
And— SOLD; —to-the-gentleman-with-the-bald-head-for-one-dollar!"

Sometime ago, someone sent me a copy of another old auction bill that I have reread with a laugh many times since. Here's a shorter version of it:

---

### LOSING OUT SALE
Having been asked to leave the county, I will sell to the highest bidder at my farm, (the Sheriff can give you the location) on
SOMDAY, May B, 1930
Beginning promptly at 1:30 g.m., the following property, N.G.

### HORSES—MULES, etc.

One spavined mare, coming twenty; 1 bay horse, weight about 400; 1 baying dog; 1 saw horse, works single or double; 1 grey gelding, blind in one eye; 1 sorrel horse; completely broken; 1 running hourse, has glanders; 1 mare mule with cold by side; 1 wicked filly, has poll evil; 1 Jack with measley points and smooth mouth, sired about 15 years ago by nobody knows who, but damned by everybody ever since.

### COWS—CATTLE

12 milch cows, all good kickers and some good milkers; 7 yearling heifers, coming three in the spring; 2 brood cows with milking machines attached; 1 Poland china bull calf, soon be four.

### SHOATS—HOGS

One hired man, going on ninety, a pig for gravy; 2 old bores about 80, still spry.

### FARM AND HOME MACHINERY

One rolling pin, tested hard wood; 1 sewing machine, a Singer, and 1 Canary, also a singer; 1 tractor with mortgage attachments; 2 bull rakes, 1 bull fiddle, a lot of bull frogs and a go-devil; 1 sulky rake and 1 sulky wife: 1 Deere plow and other dear machinery; 1 talking-machine, mother-in-law variety; 1 side board in the house and one on the wagon, makes two; 1 saw-buck and one buck-saw—neither saw will saw but both bucks will buck.

### OTHER ODDS AND ENDS

One Hampshire ram, with detachable rims; 2 ewes with little wees by side; several other sheep and a quantity of sheep sorrel; 1 Billy goat, a goatee and three Nannies; 2 swarms of bees and a cattle pony that has the hives; 1 barrow fit to butcher, and 1 wheelbarrow fit for nothing; 1 Durock rooster with more pip than pep; 4 dozen Delusion hens, some sitting, some setting, some laying and some lieing; 2 dozen spring pullets, just going into their second molt; 1 single comb Jersey Red hired girl— (Some Chicken) .

LUNCH: It will be after dinner when you come, and before supper when you go, so just forget about that.

COL. H. I. PRICE, Auctioneer
M. Y. BANKER, Clerk

I. B. GOING, Owner

-----------------------------------------------------------------

\* \* \*

But while auctions are interesting places to observe human nature in action and occasionally to get a good laugh, they are seldom funny to the owners who are selling out.

Some years ago, I happened to go into the house where an elderly couple—friends of mine—were selling their lifetime possessions. In an upstairs room, sitting alone on a single chair, the only piece of furniture left in the room was the old lady weeping as if her heart was broken, as indeed it nearly was. She had been born on that place, had married there, and she and her husband had been partners with her father until her parents had died. After that, they carried on the farm business for a good part of their lifetime. But now the old couple had come to the end of the road. They were physically unable to work the farm and were going to live with a married daughter in the city.

Being sold from the front porch were the old lady's personal possessions with which she had always lived. When I put my arm around her bent shoulders, she said to me with a catch in her voice: "Eddie, I just couldn't stand it to stay out there and listen to the auctioneer make jokes and hear the crowd laugh when things that I have always loved were going into the hands of strangers."

Life is a series of constant changes, involving the need to make difficult adjustments. I have a deep sympathy for older people who are forced by change and age to make a complete adjustment and try to make a new life—a life different from what they have always known.

# CHAPTER TWENTY-THREE

# THE GREAT AWAKENING

### THE FARMER'S INSTITUTES AND COUNTY AGENTS

WHEN I WAS A VERY YOUNG BOY, FATHER TOOK ME to a neighborhood meeting in a little one-room schoolhouse where a man talked about ways of improving farming. That was the first Farmers' Institute held in the neighborhood, and the man was an institute lecturer from the New York State College of Agriculture.

During the course of the evening, the lecturer talked about the miracle of alfalfa as a wonderful legume, high in protein. When he had finished, an old farmer jumped to his feet and, addressing his son, shouted, "Lennie, when you git home, you feed them hogs some alfalfa hay."

I don't remember the event but I do remember my folks laughing about it afterwards. The lecturer was years ahead of his time, as most pioneers are, for there was not a spear of alfalfa grown in the neighborhood at the time, and probably very little in the whole county. The farmers there would not have recognized the alfalfa if they had seen it, let alone having had any experience in growing it.

Yet that event did prove something, I think. It showed the receptiveness of that farmer, and thousands of others across America, to the new science of agriculture, which, coupled with the astounding increase in the invention and use of farm machinery since the Civil War, has completely transformed America and our way of life.

When President Abraham Lincoln, 100 years ago, signed the bill creating the land grant colleges in the United States, he set in motion the wheels of agricultural science, which have turned faster and faster with each succeeding year and have changed agriculture from a haphazard nonscientific occupation to one of the most complicated scientific professions in the world. The Farmers' Institutes were a vital part of this movement of carrying scientific

John Barron—the first county agent in the United States—shows James Quinn, the first county Farm Bureau president, seed treatment for disease (1912).

information from the colleges of agriculture, home economics, and experimental stations to the people. The Institutes were the beginning of farm extension work, now reaching millions of farm, town, and city homes across the land.

It was my privilege to know many of those Farmers' Institute instructors or lecturers, the last of whom was Jared Van Wagenen, Jr., of Lawyersville, N. Y., who died in 1960. I was one of the early county agents (or farm bureau managers, as they were called in my state).

The County Farm Bureau succeeded and somewhat overlapped the last of the Farmers' Institutes. That's how new the whole extension movement is which we now take for granted.

President A. S. Welch of the Iowa State College organized and conducted the first Farmers' Institutes in the United States. Among those associated with him as Institute instructors was Isaac Phillips Roberts, later the first dean of the College of Agriculture at Cornell University. In his book, *Autobiography of a Farm Boy,* published by the Cornell University Press, Roberts says:

Our experiences were those of pioneers. On one such occasion after an evening meeting at Council Bluffs, Iowa, the President and I were invited to go home with a farmer who lived five miles distant. About midnight, we retired to a room on the walls of which you might have written your name in the glittering frost. I slept with the President and when we reached the icy sheets, he remarked: 'Roberts, I guess we will have to spoon'—and we spooned.

A brief history of how the Institutes worked in New York State will illustrate in a general way how farm and home extension work originated and was carried on in most states. The first Farmers' Institute in New York State was held at the New York State College of Agriculture at Cornell University for three days in February 1886, only three-quarters of a century ago. That's how rapidly the farmers have awakened and used the principles of scientific agriculture in the production of food and fiber.

To reach the Institute meetings, the hardy pioneer speakers, lecturers, laymen, and college professors traveled by horse and buggy or sleigh for long distances, through all kinds of weather, and put up sometimes with almost impossible accommodations. In writing about a woman lecturer, one of her companions reported: "She was always a good sport; she accepted such hardships as long cold drives behind slow teams and frigid bedrooms in country hotels

206

The county home bureau agent demonstrates the latest canning tricks to
a group of farm women.

with cheerful optimism as being just a part of the
day's work while her bubbling comments on folks
and things made her a merry comrade."

The program of the Farmers' Institutes often extended over four or five days, with long forenoon and
afternoon and evening sessions. Some attempt was
made to vary the program with music or other entertainment, and good meals were served.

That the Institutes came at the right time and
filled a need is proven by the fact that they were well
attended, and that the farmers and their wives
stayed through those long sessions. One fact that

accounted for the good attendance was that there was little entertainment in the neighborhoods in those times, so the Institutes broke the monotony when there was nothing to do in the winter on the farm except to cut wood and do the chores.

From those first meetings, Farmers' Institutes spread rapidly, until by the end of 1909 there was a total annual attendance of 200,000 people with local meetings in every farm county in the state.

It has been said that the Farmers' Institute lecturer put more emphasis on farming as a way of life than he did on scientific facts. To that I answer, "Why not?" Today, we have swung to the other extreme with practically *all* the emphasis, both in our farm journals and in the extension work, on commercialism. This is necessary, of course, but only part of the story. It is certainly as important to know *how* to live happily as it is to make a living. That's one reason why I have always been interested in homemaking or home demonstration, as well as in agriculture extension work.

This home bureau work has grown in popularity almost as fast as has extension work in agriculture and is equally as important. Not only has extension work in homemaking courses helped women in the practical knowledge of how to run a home and feed and clothe their family, but, what is more important, it has given the homemaker the point of view that homemaking is the greatest and most important profession in the world.

To extension work in agriculture and homemaking, there was soon added the equally important work of the 4-H clubs, with their paid county agents, in the majority of rural counties in the United States and the tremendous membership of rural boys and girls learning the science and practice of agriculture and homemaking. No one can ever measure what the 4-H work, together with that of vocational agriculture in the high schools and the Future Farmers, has done and is doing for America. As long as enough young people join and take an active part in these fine organizations, the future of rural America will be safe.

So let us pause to pay our respects to those pioneer leaders in the Farmers' Institutes and similar organizations across the United States, who laid the foundations for the extension work of the farm and home bureaus and the 4-H clubs. They have brought agriculture and homemaking know-how to every farm community in the country, and have done and are doing so much to feed and clothe the people.

Following closely on the heels of the Farmers' Institutes came the first County Farm Bureau in the United States, organized in Broome County in 1911 by the Binghamton Chamber of Commerce, the Delaware and Lackawanna Railroad, and the office of Farm Management of the Bureau of Plant Industry of the United States Department of Agriculture. Mr. John H. Barron was the first county agricultural agent employed to work in Broome and adjacent counties.

The New York State College of Agriculture was not permitted under the law to furnish funds, but acted as a general supervisor. The board of supervisors of Broome County soon began making appropriations for the work.

In connection with the growth of extension work, it is interesting to recall personal experiences of Day Before Yesterday when I was an early county agent in a large New York farm county. To accept the job, I left the position as teacher of agriculture in the middle of the winter of 1915 to begin work on the job that few people, including myself, knew much about.

Like the Farmers' Institute lecturer, the early county agent pioneered in county extension work and tried to take up where the Farmers' Institutes left off, although some Institute work was still being done.

In spite of the fact that our first meetings were poorly attended and that there was still great resistance to "book larnin'," many leading farmers were beginning to realize that it was impossible to continue to make a living without more scientific knowledge. So sometimes I drove as far as 75 miles to attend a meeting of perhaps not more than eight or 10 persons to discuss or demonstrate some new or better varieties of crops, better seeds or fertilizer practices, or what have you. But those eight or 10 people were interested enough to make my trip worthwhile, and they formed the nucleus and the leadership in their neighborhoods that insured a larger meeting and more interest the next time.

At that time, there were only a few miles of paved roads in that large county, and the journeys—materially and spiritually—were long, lonely, and often

This was the Marsh harvester used in 1858. Two men riding on the apron of the machine bound the grain with straw binders as fast it was cut.

The mowing machine succeeding the sickle and the scythe was in common use Day Before Yesterday.

Whetting the cradle blade in good company.

Haying time. The hay was cut by a mowing machine, raked by one like in the picture, bunched into hay cocks by hand and pitched to the man on the load, then carried to the barn where it usually was pitched into the mow by hand and mowed away up under the barn or shed roof—just about the hottest place on earth.

A study in contrasts. When I was county agent in Delaware County, N.Y. in 1916, I led a Farm Bureau parade of cars, oxen, and trucks to demonstrate agricultural extension work. Those are the Catskill Mountains in the background.

discouraging. But today, in retrospect, the well-supported extension work, the farm and home bureaus, and the 4-H clubs to be found in nearly every farm county in the United States, make all the discouragement of earlier days seem well worthwhile.

But county agent work in the early days, with all of its problems, had its good moments and its light ones. Precious indeed are the memories of the friend-ships in that county which, to this day, make returning there seem like going back home. The Catskill Mountains spill over into the county, so that strangers riding through might wonder why it is one of the largest and most intensive dairy counties in the United States. With its steep hills, how are the farmers able to pasture their cows and raise their crops? The answer is—the above-average rainfall. The farmers there used to tell me that they had to grow cows with two legs shorter on one side than the other so that the cows could walk or feed across the pasture with the short legs on the upper side to keep their balance.

A typical story of this county is about the stranger who was driving along the road and saw a man roll off a hillside and land in the road ahead of him. The stranger jumped out of his wagon and ran to see if the man was hurt. The farmer got slowly to his feet, grunting and groaning, and exclaimed, "Mister, I'm gettin' pretty nigh discouraged. That's the fourth time I've fallen out of my cornfield this morning!"

## THE VILLAGE LECTURE COURSES —THEY FILLED A NEED

Nothing in my high-school days more aroused my enthusiasm and determination to set goals and achieve them than did the village lecture courses that were in operation in my home town and in thousands of other towns and cities Day Before Yesterday.

As long as I live, I shall remember Russell H. Conwell's lecture, "Acres of Diamonds," which he delivered thousands of times and which inspired hun-

The late Liberty Hyde Bailey, dean of the New York State College of Agriculture, farmer, scientist, writer, one of the great pioneer leaders in agricultural teaching and extension.

dreds of thousands of his listeners. From the proceeds of this lecture, Conwell helped to establish the great Temple University of Philadelphia.

Conwell's theme in "Acres of Diamonds" was similar to Tennyson's in the "Holy Grail." Both emphasize the fact that men so often spend and ruin their lives searching for the will-o'-the-wisp or the

213

gold at the end of the rainbow, when in truth it can often be found right in their own backyards. "The pasture always looks greener over the fence."

Respect is due to the many thousands of leading citizens in the small towns of the United States who provided the leadership and courage to give the lyceum or lecture courses and underwrite them financially, sometimes at considerable loss. For example, the Chautauqua Committee in my home town was composed of the editor of the local country weekly, the president of the board of education, the principal of the high school, from one to several of the pastors, the local supervisor, and others—all public-minded leaders of the community who wanted the best for their friends and neighbors. Such leaders brought to the community nationally-known leturers and musical organizations at a time when there was little other public entertainment of high cultural value.

Of course, the public lecture is an old institution, going back into our early history. For example, no public speaker was ever greater or more thrilling than Daniel Webster. Oratory and the public forum, where men aired their views and controversies, were always an important form of communication. But the lecture bureau or lyceum, as we of my generation knew it, had its heyday after the Civil War, and ended with the coming of motion pictures and the automobile.

About 1867, James Redpath, a former newspaperman, organized the Boston Lyceum Bureau, later renamed Redpath Lyceum Bureau, which led the way to the hundreds of lecture courses throughout the country. There were many other bureau organizations, but none was able to secure the talent that Redpath booked for his lectures. Included were Anna Elizabeth Dickinson, Julia Ward Howe, Mark Twain (Samuel Clemens), Petroleum V. Nasby (David Ross Locke), Ralph Waldo Emerson, Henry Thoreau, and Josh Billings (Henry Wheeler Shaw).

In addition to those already mentioned, there were many other famous personalities on the lecture bureau circuit, right down into the first years of the twentieth century. One was Horace Greeley, who became so popular that Ralph Waldo Emerson, the poet, in writing of his own lack of audience said: "Greeley preceded me by a few days and the people gathered together to come 30 or 40 miles to hear him speak."

James Whitcomb Riley and Eugene Field, the Hoosier poets, made the lecture circuit, sometimes speaking from the same platform with Edgar (Bill) Wilson Nye. It is said that the three of them could make an audience laugh or cry almost at will.

In these days when an audience begins to get tired of a speech more than 15 or 20 minutes long, one wonders how the old-time orators held their audiences spellbound for as long as two hours sometimes. Horace Greeley is reported to have said that he could always tell when his audience got tired, for they just got up and left! There were two reasons, I think, why people listened so long. First, there was little or no entertainment in those times, and second, there was the tremendous personality and delivery of many of the giants who served on the lecture platform.

A glance at the list of lecturers mentioned proves my point. The lecture courses and the Farmers' Institutes were a part of The Great Awakening which began to stir Americans and which helped to lay the foundations Day Before Yesterday for the new social and economic life of today.

# CHAPTER TWENTY-FOUR

# WHO SAYS FARMERS CAN'T ORGANIZE?

NEWTOWN 10 MI.

GRANGE HALL 5 MI.

ONE OF THE MOST IMPORTANT EVENTS OF THE Great Awakening that has taken place in America since the Civil War, and especially since 1900, is the organization of society into groups. In the city, this has been in the form of labor unions, in the country, in farm organizations and cooperatives. In the city, economic conditions, the long working day, and the often unfair low wages forced workers to join unions for self-protection. It was the same in the country. The changing economic situation made it more and more difficult for the individual farmer to make a living.

Since I have had some small part in the farm organization movement, perhaps a brief review of the facts with comments from my personal experience and viewpoint will be interesting. I have been a member of the Grange for 50 years, I was one of the early Farm Bureau managers, or county agents, and an executive in the first days of one of the largest milk marketing cooperatives.

Of course, there have been some small farm clubs, agricultural societies, and associations of farmers from the earliest years of our history. Some of these had considerable power and influence; for example, the New York State Agricultural Society, founded in 1832 and still functioning, had a large part in influencing the farm affairs of the state for many years. But it was not until after the Civil War, when farming began to turn more and more from a self-sufficient occupation to dependence upon the markets, that farm organizations began to get their real start.

It would take volumes to describe the organized farm groups in any detail, but in the following pages I have tried to give you some of the high-spots.

Organized farmers may be grouped into two general classifications: the first, the great *nationwide organizations*, with their state and local groups, known as the Grange or the Patrons of Husbandry, The Farm-

ers Educational and Cooperative Union of America (Farmers Union), and the American Farm Bureau Federation (AFBF); the second, the *cooperatives* engaged in buying farm supplies for their members or selling their products. Some of these groups also are federated or organized on a regional or national basis.

## THE GRANGE LED THE WAY

Few organizations have had a greater part in the Great Awakening since the Civil War than the Grange. Right after the war, impressed with the terrible economic and social conditions in the South, President Andrew Johnson sent Oliver H. Kelley, a midwestern farmer, then working in Washington, into the South to study the situation there, especially its agriculture. From this study, it was hoped that some constructive plan for assistance could be formulated. Kelley came back to Washington, but instead of recommending measures that the Government might take, he founded, in 1867, a self-help organization which he called the Grange, or the Patrons of Husbandry.

It was Kelley's thought that the Grange could help unite the people of the South and help them to

The late Governor Franklin D. Roosevelt signing an important rural bill with Henry Morgentheau, Jr. (seated) and farm leaders of New York State.

educate themselves in the principles of scientific agriculture, and through a well-supported organization make their influence felt in the states and the nation for the good of farming and farmers.

The Grange immediately took hold and grew rapidly; and while it has had its ups and downs in its long history of nearly 100 years, it is still one of the three largest and most powerful rural organizations in the United States. Unlike the Farmer's Union and the Farm Bureau, the Grange is a secret order, following a ritual somewhat similar to the Masonic Order.

Strange to say, while it was Kelley's idea to make the Grange a great, powerful, and helpful influence in the South, it never flourished there, but instead became large and powerful in the North. The first Grange was founded by Kelley in Washington in 1868, and was known as Potomac Grange No. 1. The organization has four divisions: the Subordinate, or Local Granges in the communities and the villages; the Pomona, which is formed from Subordinate Granges of the county; the State Grange, composed of the Subordinate and Pomona Granges; and finally the National Grange, representing the other divisions and members.

Most excellent, indeed, is the record of achievements made by the Grange in influencing local, state, and national legislation, not only good for farmers, but good for everybody. Some of the Grange accomplishments made alone, or in cooperation with others, was its pioneer work in helping to establish the R.F.D., the Parcel Post, and good roads. The Grange supported the founding and maintenance of Agricultural Colleges and Experiment Stations. Its support of the woman's suffrage movement was a natural one, because women are received as members in the Grange on an equal basis with men, as they should be. Some other achievements of the Grange include the support of postal savings banks, and a continuing fight against the liquor traffic. Equally effective with its national work, the State and Subordinate Granges have been powerful with state and local legislation.

The Grange has sometimes opposed progressive measures, but even here, perhaps, its influence was in the main helpful, because new proposals need sometimes to be slowed down in order to prevent mistakes which would have to be corrected later. Several times in its history, the Grange has attempted to enter the commercial field, almost always without lasting success. In recent years, the organization has found that the best way to help farmers commercially is by supporting cooperative organizations like the farmers' life, accident, and fire insurance companies, and individual organizations like the G.L.F. (Grange, Dairymen's League, Farm Bureau). Testifying to the continuing interest and strength of the Grange, there are in the United States as of this date (1963) approximately 800,000 Grangers.

One of the most important of the Grange contributions was in helping farmers to express themselves, to get on their feet and discuss their problems and points of view in public. Their conclusions are then put in the form of resolutions, are brought to the attention of the State and National Grange, and through them to the State and Federal Governments.

At one time I served as a lecturer of a Subordinate Grange, with the responsibility of providing the program. Our programs at that time are typical of others in thousands of Subordinate Granges across America. For fun we had mock trials, spelling matches, musical programs, and, oh, yes, let's not forget the eats. It still makes my mouth water to think of those Grange feasts, where the women vied with one another to bring in the most delicious home-baked pies and cakes, where the tables were loaded with just about everything that can be grown on a Northern farm, and where you ate and ate and ate, because you didn't dare skip any of the cakes while the owner's eye was on you. Then you went home and rolled and tumbled the rest of the night wondering what was the matter with you. The trouble, of course, was not with the quality of the food, but the quantity you had consumed.

In one of the mock trials we put on, I was tried for chicken stealing—and they convicted me, too! The principal of their own high school.

But it was not all fun. The many discussions and debates were hot and heavy. Both the men and women forgot to be self-conscious in their earnestness to make their points and get their arguments across. These discussions ranged through the entire category of local, state, and national problems that influenced the welfare and lives of the people. When you realize that similar discussions have been carried on by the people themselves, in thousands of meetings a year for nearly 100 years of Grange history, you can get some idea of the power the Grange has had, and still has, and the good that it has done.

## THE FARMERS' UNION FOR DIRECT ACTION

The Farmers' Educational and Cooperative Union of America, usually known as the Farmers' Union, is one of the three major national farm organizations. The Farmers' Union is most strongly organized in the Plain states, with its largest membership in North and South Dakota, Nebraska, Minnesota, Oklahoma,

Oliver Hudson Kelley. He founded the National Grange (Patrons of Husbandry) in 1867.

up rapidly during the farm depression of the twenties and thirties, shifting its membership from the South and the Southwest to the Plain states where the depression hit the hardest. Today, it has a membership of about 300,000.

The Farmers' Union maintains local, county, and state divisions and has succeeded better than the Farm Bureau in maintaining very similar locals throughout the states. In the twenties and thirties there was much difference of opinion among the leaders about basic policies, but much of those differences has now disappeared and the general policy is now for more direct action, including political activity and more Government help for farmers.

## THE AFBF—YOUNGEST AND LARGEST

Soon after the first Farm Bureaus were formed, they were organized in most states into State Farm Bureau Federations, which in turn joined the American Farm Bureau Federation (AFBF), organized in 1919. Because the county agricultural, homemaking, and 4-H associations with their agents are partly supported by Federal, state, and local taxes, they were

and Wisconsin; but it also has members in most of the other states.

Organized in 1903, with its greatest strength at first in the South and Southwest, it soon had 18,000 locals. An entire family is counted as one member of the Farmers' Union. The number of members declined rapidly during World War I, but picked unable ethically to engage in commercial activities. They are therefore entirely separated from the Farm Bureaus which, like the Grange and the Farmers' Union, are now independent farm organizations. However, the Farm Burean has always worked closely with the state college and experiment stations in their educational programs.

The Central states have the largest Farm Bureau membership and strength, although the Farm Bureau is national in scope and has a large and active membership in many other states, such as New York.

Although the AFBF is the youngest of the large national farm organizations, it is also the largest, with a membership of about 1,607,505 farm families out of about 6,000,000 farms in the United States in 1962. Because the Farm Bureau Federations have always placed emphasis on economic problems, their membership goes down rapidly in hard times. In comparison with the Grange and the Farmers' Union, it may be said that the AFBF is a middle-road organization in its policy. It is more economic than the Grange and not as socially inclined. The policies of the AFBF are developed on the basis of the wishes and resolutions of the county and state organizations. Although farmers in different parts of the United States hold widely differing viewpoints, depending on local conditions, the AFBF has been remarkably successful in reconciling and compromising these differences, so that, generally, the organization has come through with a well-organized and well-supported policy. The list of the work and achievements of the Farm Bureau Federation is remarkably long.

The state organizations, either under their own name or through subsidiaries, are very successful in conducting various commercial enterprises such as insurance, farm supplies, the support of farmer cooperatives, and other farm marketing associations.

Possibly the most important achievement of the AFBF and of the state organizations has been through their influence *for or against* legislation affecting the interests of farm people. Time and again, both nationally and in the states, the farm bureau has been successful in preventing the passage of laws *not* in the interests of farmers, and in promoting bills good not only for farmers but for everybody.

One of the most interesting kinds of local Farm

Bureau meetings is the "Kitchen Conference," organized by the New York State Farm Buren in hundreds of communities throughout the state. As the name implies, local farmers gather in small groups, often in the kitchens of farm homes, to discuss in an organized way their social and economical problems—local, state, and national. Their conclusions are reported to the county annual meeting and become a part of the Farm Bureau's state and national program—for legislation or other action.

In some cases, each of the three units (county agriculture, home economics, and 4-H) has its own board of directors and officers, and in some cases they join in an overhead county organization of the three units with its board and officers. All together, this extension system, which to some degree varies in organization in the different states, makes one of the largest and most effective educational organizations in the United States.

Of the three largest general farm organizations, it may be said that the American Farm Bureau Federation (AFBF) is the most conservative in its policies. The Farmers' Union is the most liberal, while the National Grange, in general, is somewhere between the other two, although in recent years the Grange leadership seems to be leaning more to liberal policies.

Of the three organizations, the Farmers' Union is nearest in policy to that of union labor. All three organizations, through their thousands of local meetings, try to educate farmers in production and marketing problems, and especially by developing cooperatives. The Union goes farther than the other two national organizations in urging that farmers eliminate dealers and middle men and take their products directly to the consumer.

The Farmers' Union, through its cooperatives, would restore ownership of land to the operators, provide crop and other insurance, build processing plants, and manufacture farm machinery.

The three great national organizations—Farmers' Union, National Grange, and the Farm Bureau Federation—have not been able to do as much as they could for farmers socially, economically, or in terms of legislation, because of wide differences of opinion and lack of cooperation among the leaders of the different groups. No wonder Congressional and state legislative leaders are confused as to what farmers want and what they should have. Of course, farmers themselves differ widely in different sections of the country, so it is perhaps natural for their leaders to differ. Nevertheless, I think it is unfortunate that farmers can't speak with one voice on at least some fundamental problems of concern to all of them.

This situation is especially unfortunate since the number of farmers has now grown so relatively small that they are far outnumbered, politically and economically, by consumers, who are naturally interested in low food prices.

However, in fairness, it should be said that in spite of this lack of cooperation, the three major farm organizations have done much good and farmers would be in far worse condition without them.

Probably the most important contribution of all the farm organizations, since most of them started Day Before Yesterday, is the help they have given farmers to express themselves publicly. Unlucky is the speaker who attempts to address a farm audience now if he is not well armed with the facts. The farmer has always been a thinker. Now he does not hesitate to put his thoughts into words, and he knows how to raise his voice in meetings to ask questions and state opinions vigorously. In this, the farmer is a good example for all the rest of us.

# CHAPTER TWENTY-FIVE

# THE FARMER
# IN THE MARKET PLACE

FROM THE CLOSE OF THE CIVIL WAR UNTIL THE present time, there have been few periods, none of them very long, when the majority of American farmers have been really prosperous. In times of general prosperity, prices for farm products have been the last to go up, and the first to go down at the approach of a recession or depression.

The very richness of our natural resources, like the fertility of our soil, has caused an abundance of food and fiber, resulting in surpluses that have kept farm prices down. It has been said, with some truth, that one cause of the Industrial Revolution and the rapid growth of our cities since the Civil War has been the low price of food. To some extent at least,

225

the cities have been built on this abundance, from which the farmer generally has not profited. With the use of the modern farm equipment and the application of science, the consumer still continues to profit from low food prices compared to his income, whereas the farmer continues to suffer financially from the resulting food surpluses.

As a farm boy, around the turn of the century, my earliest and strongest impression is of the struggle my parents and practically all the other farmers had to make both ends meet. When the expenses were paid, there seldom was enough left over from the milk check to give the family any more than the bare necessities of life. And those necessities were darn few compared to what we think is necessary now.

Our small income from the dairy was supplemented by a few acres of potatoes we raised. When the crop was good, the price was down. I have myself sold potatoes for 10 cents a bushel. If, by good fortune, we had a fair crop and got a fair price, then we could count on warm clothes and boots for the winter. These conditions early impressed me with the fact that, if there was anything that really needed doing in America, it was to help get more financial security for the farmer. Because of their often desperate struggle to make both ends meet, there was a seething unrest, especially among dairymen who had changed from butter-making to shipping fluid milk to the rapidly growing cities. Time and again, dairymen tried to organize neighborhood cooperatives in order to get a better price for their milk. Few of them ever succeeded, because milk buyers would temporarily raise the price of milk to farmers around the cooperatives. Then the dairymen would desert their cooperative to get the better prices, only to find that they were soon right back with their poor prices after their cooperative had been forced to close its doors.

## DAIRYMEN IN THE MARKET PLACE

As one example of what farmers have tried to do to improve their markets, let me describe, mostly from first-hand experience, a fairly typical, large group of dairymen organized to sell their products. This is the Dairymen's League Cooperative Association, located in the five states known as the New York milk shed (New York, northern Pennsylvania, northern New Jersey, western Vermont, and western Connecticut).

In 1894, some dairymen who were selling fluid milk to New York City organized what they called the Five States Milk Producers Association. My father joined this cooperative. Then its officers called a strike to withhold their milk from the market in the month of June, when there is more milk available than at any other time in the year. The dealers were easily able to get all the milk they wanted from dairymen who were not members of the association, and the whole effort collapsed. My father and hundreds of other members would never have anything to do with cooperative marketing again.

But conditions among dairymen continued to grow worse until, finally, another group of milk shippers in Orange County, New York, close to the big New York City market, organized in 1907 the Dairymen's League. For years, this association made very slow progress. Then, in the spring of 1916, its officers announced that, as of October of that year, the price of all milk in the five states known as the New York City milk shed would be set at a figure very materially higher than the prices offered by the dealers.

World War I had started; the farmer's expenses were rapidly increasing, with little or no increase for what he was producing. Dairymen had reached the limit of their endurance, so they joined the Dairymen's League so fast and in such numbers that the officers, taken by surprise, were hardly able to keep up their records. On October 1, 1916, the dealers having refused to pay the League prices, the League ordered their members to withhold . their milk from the market. There was tremendous excitement. I know, because I was there! I was a county agricultural agent, or Farm Bureau manager, in one of the largest dairy counties in the United States.

I do not believe in strikes—at least not until every other possibility has been exhausted—but, as I have stated, it had been ground into my soul in my earliest years that farmers were getting the short end of the deal much of the time. So I risked my job and my reputation to go all out in supporting the dairymen in their great efforts to get a living price for their milk. During the two weeks while the strike lasted, I attended some three or four meetings of dairymen a day to get them to join the League and withhold their milk. While the battle raged, there was much bitterness, but, I am glad to say, little violence. Many dairymen realized that they *had* to have better prices

227

or go out of business. They got better prices—the dealers gave in. When I got the telegram from Albert Manning, the Dairymen's League secretary, stating that the organization had won, I jumped clear over my office desk—much to the consternation of my secretary, who thought I had lost what little brains I had.

Within a few weeks after the League had secured the prices the dairymen had demanded, the membership of the cooperative jumped to approximately 100,000 dairymen, comprising a very large majority of all the fluid-milk producers in the New York City milk shed. After World War I, the League changed its set-up to include the ownership of milk plants for both the manufacture of milk into its by-products, and for shipping some of it in fluid form to the markets. The membership now (1963) is 17,000.

About the same time as the Dairymen's League success, the dairymen around Chicago, in similar straits, organized a Chicago milk producers' association, which was successful in materially raising the milk prices for its members.

The success of the producers in the New York and Chicago milk sheds quickly led to the organization of milk producers supplying milk to practically every major American city. Unfortunately for dairymen in several of these milk sheds, differences of opinion arose among their leaders, resulting in more than one cooperative organizing in the same milk shed.

Most of the milk producers' cooperatives, similar to the Dairymen's League Associations, joined in an overhead organization known as the National Milk Producers Federation, with headquarters in Washington, D.C. This group acts on legislation and policy affecting all dairymen.

At about the same time that the dairymen formed cooperatives, farmers producing other commodities formed similar organizations, until today there are approximately 10,000 cooperative marketing associations covering just about everything the farmer has for sale.

Organizing in an effort to get better prices for his products helped to solve only one part of the farmer's problem in the market place. Even though he might partially succeed in getting better prices for what he sold, he still faced a problem that he thought was equally difficult—paying overly high prices for the increasing amount of supplies he had to use in his rapidly growing modern business.

When the farmers had been nearly self-sufficient, raising and processing most of their food and fiber on their own farms, including feed for the poultry and cattle, prices in the market place had not made too much difference. But now, all that had changed. Farming had become a commercial enterprise, and if the farmer was to stay in business, he must get a living price for what he sold and keep his costs down by not paying exorbitant prices for what he bought. Counting all he was now buying, both for operating his farm and for his home, the farmer and his family rapidly became more and more of a consumer.

To meet this situation, many attempts were made at group or cooperative buying, most of which failed for lack of enough members or leadership. Although the farmer is a skilled producer, he had little skill at first either in directing or operating a buying cooperative. Gradually, however, farmers learned by their failures and began to acquire some skill both in selling and buying.

## HOW THE G.L.F. WORKS

While there are now many successful purchasing cooperatives, let's visit for a moment about one of the largest and most successful farmers' purchasing cooperatives in the world—the Cooperative Grange League Federation Exchange, Inc., more commonly known as the G.L.F.

In order to meet the increasing need of buying high-quality supplies at reasonable prices, the New York State Grange organized in 1918, the Grange Exchange as a separate stock corporation; purchase of stock, however, was limited to Grange members. The purpose of the Exchange was to purchase for the farmers in wholesale lots and at reduced prices, mainly dairy and poultry feeds, seed, and fertilizer.

But while the Grange Exchange met with some success, it left much to be desired and it was soon realized that it needed more support and bigger volume. So an approach was made to the leaders of the Dairymen's League and the New York State Federation of Farm Bureaus to set up a farmers' purchasing cooperative that would have the support of the three major organizations in the state. As a result, the Grange Exchange was reorganized at Syracuse, New York, in June 1920, under the name of the Grange League Federation—G.L.F. Two of the three organizations still nominate directors of the G.L.F. board, but the organizations themselves have no legal control over G.L.F.

Almost from the start, the cooperative flourished. It adopted policies insisting on the highest possible quality of products, with the ingredients always made known to farmers through open formulas. The G.L.F. has been particularly fortunate in acquiring a wise and efficient personnel—from its board of directors and general managers, to its hundreds of employees throughout the territory, which includes New York, New Jersey, and part of Pennsylvania. As of its last annual report for the fiscal year ending June 30, 1962, there are 242 local cooperatives owned and controlled by farmers which the G.L.F. operates for them under a management contract.

G.F.L. supplies almost everything the farmer uses except heavy farm machinery. The organization is also doing an increasing amount of farm produce marketing. It has an enthusiastic membership of 117,000, and employs 4,200 people in its headquarters in Ithaca, its other offices, and in its wholesale and retail operations in its three-state area. During the fiscal year of 1961–62, it did a wholesale business of $196,000,000, of which about $31,700,000 was for products marketed for patrons. Sales by the 242 local cooperatives totaled $122,000,000, and retail petroleum volume was $30,000,000.

The G.L.F. is only one example, of course, of the many farmers' purchasing cooperatives in the United States. If you add together the total business done by all cooperatives—both for selling the farmers' products and buying their supplies—you can get some idea of the remarkable progress made by the American farmers in the market place in about 50 years.

Many of these cooperatives of both kinds belong to an overhead national organization with headquarters in Washington, D.C., known as the Council of Farmer Cooperatives. Affiliated with the Council are local, state, regional, and national cooperatives, which range in size from a few hundred to several hundred thousand members. The Council actually represents 5,700 associations, more than half of all the cooperatives in America, which serve a farmer membership of nearly three million farmers as of 1962.

In the words of the Council itself, it stands ready at all times to join with other agricultural organizations and community groups in developing and coordinating policies, and fostering the interest of all American agriculture.

I might add that the constructive policies of almost all of the independent cooperatives and of the National Council are not only in the interests of the farmers themselves but of *everybody,* for our economy is based on a successful and prosperous agriculture.

Although I believe in these farmer cooperatives and organizations and admire the excellent job that most of them are doing, I hope the time will never come when they will have a monopoly on all of the selling of farm products or the purchasing of supplies. There is still a very necessary place for the independent dealer. Each system keeps the farmer on his toes, and both the farmer and the consumer benefit from the competition.

To be sure, the farmer and his organizations have not made all the progress they should, either in the market place or in the political halls, because too often they have not been able to speak with one voice, with the result that legislators are often confused as to what farmers *really do want and need.* In a nation as large and as diverse as ours, perhaps it is expecting too much that all farmers and their leaders should always agree. Sometimes interests in different sections of the country are diametrically opposed, even among those producing the same product. However, in spite of disagreement and competition among leaders of the cooperatives, they have done an outstanding job and have built constructive and worthwhile organizations. As a result, the farmers themselves are far better off today than they were during the chaotic days that I can remember, when they had few or no cooperatives. Without the cooperative organizations, there surely would be chaos in the complicated farm marketing business.

The farmer has won, in a short time, a real standing in the market place!

# CHAPTER TWENTY-SIX

# FAMILY STORIES

### "A HOG IS A HOG"

I ALWAYS GET A LAUGH WHEN I THINK OF MY father with a pail of swill in one hand and a stick in the other, leaning over the wall of the pig-pen trying to dump the swill into the trough on the inside, before the crowding hogs, in their eagerness to eat, knocked the pail out of his hands. On many such occasions, I have heard Father say with great emphasis, "A hog *is* a hog!" Anyone who has ever tried to feed hogs under similar circumstances will know just what Father meant. Certainly there is no other living creature so crazy to eat, so hoggish, as a hog. Yet, strange to say, a hog is the only farm animal that will not overeat if given the opportunity. Horses, for example, if they get access to a grain bin, will kill themselves.

Driving home the cows has always been a daily farm chore in the summertime, but I regret now that we lazy boys too often let father do it.

As every farmer knows, there are often more pigs born in a litter than there are places at the "dinner table." So one pig, called the titman, is usually crowded and bullied by the others until he fails to grow or, as is often the case, is taken to the house and artificially fed and cared for.

A fact that is not usually known, even by farmers, is that the hog is rated by animal psychologists as one of the most intelligent of animals, ranking far above the cow, sheep, and horse. A pig does not often get a chance to show how smart he is because he is butchered before he gets very old. How smart would the

233

human race be if we were all killed when very young? I had a cousin who had a titman which became a real pet. He was easily housebroken and my cousin taught him many tricks. In the fall, when he had grown big and fat, my cousin's pet was butchered with the rest of the hogs, and from that day, my cousin would never eat another piece of pork. As pork used to be the chief meat in the diet, my cousin's diet must have been slim pickings.

Not only are hogs intelligent—and if you don't get run over when they are trying to get something to eat—they are usually gentle creatures. But I'll never forget one that wasn't.

To raise tuition money which farm boys and girls or their parents used to have to pay to go to high school, I bought a sow one year and made a deal with my father to feed her for half of her pigs. A sow's gestation period is 16 weeks. Time never passed so slowly as it did during those 16 weeks before those pigs were born. But they were worth waiting for. She finally had a big litter—my half of which helped me to go to school.

One day when the pigs were about six weeks old, a neighbor came to buy one. An older brother climbed into the sow's pen and picked up a pig, which, characteristically, began to squeal as if it was being murdered. That aroused the mother sow, who rushed at my brother. He dropped the little pig and jumped for a rafter over the pen. Now, ordinarily, he could never have reached that rafter, but fear added about three feet to an ordinary jump, so that he caught the rafter and pulled himself up between the rafters through the hole that led to the platform overhead. Sad to relate, he was not quite quick enough. The sow caught the seat of his pants and took them off quicker than you can "spit." Afterwards, the neighbor and I somehow diverted the sow's attention, got the pig out, and I was paid for it. Then my brother made me go to the house and get another pair of pants for him to cover his dignity. He always claimed that he should have had that pig money to pay for his ruined pants.

* * *

There was one time, more recently, when three or four of our hogs broke through their yard fence and started running around our dooryard. At that time, we had a little Boston bulldog with courage

234

much bigger than she was, and a cat which we called Old Cuss with some reason.

Almost unnaturally, Lady (our dog) and Old Cuss were firm friends, and often stood together against the world. If either was scared or in a scrape and the other knew about it, he or she would come to the rescue. Lady saw the hogs out of their yard, knew that they had no business being around there, and started on a run for them, yelping at the top of her lungs. Old Cuss, hearing the commotion, joined the fracas.

Now, swine—the four-legged variety—being just about the most obstinate critters in the world, second only to the two-legged ones, have their own ideas about things, so at first they paid no attention to the dog and cat—but not for long. Soon Old Cuss caught up with them and landed squarely on the back of one of them while the dog nipped at the hogs' heels. They set up a squealing that could be heard all over the neighborhood, and made off on a dead run with the cat still clinging to the animal's back with the dog close behind. The hogs never stopped running until they had made it through the hole in the fence back into their own yard, where their safety and security were not disturbed by all the devils of the outside world.

* * *

One cold winter morning, a neighbor who was keeping one of his sows in our hoghouse arrived to feed her and found she had given birth to a litter of 17 pigs. It was evident at a glance that she, or nature, had bitten off more than she could chew— or more, actually, than she could feed. Moreover, some of the little new-born pigs were nearly dead from the cold. The owner grabbed up the ones which seemed to be the coldest and came running to our house, where Belle put them in the warm, but not hot, oven. A little while later, miracle of miracles, the cute little things came to life—and how! They jumped out of the oven and began running all over the downstairs rooms with Belle after them. Once in a while, she succeeded in catching one and putting it back into the oven. Then she'd go back after another, only to find that the first had escaped. I guess she'd still be chasing them if the owner hadn't arrived and rescued both Belle and the pigs.

One summer, when my youngest brother was farming, he had several young growing pigs in the same pen with a big sow. When he attempted to feed them, he had the same difficulty that Father did trying to get the swill into the trough before the crowding hogs managed to spill it. He was always bothered because, if he didn't watch out, the big sow would crowd the others out and get more than her share.

Unable to drive her back one time, Albert got right over into the pen in order to get a full pail of swill into the trough. But he was out of luck. The old hog had long hair on her head, some of which came down over her eyes, partly obscuring her vision. (I've seen some hairdos recently which have the same effect.) In the mixup and in the eagerness of the sow to get into the trough, the sow, not seeing too well, crowded right between my brother's legs from in front. Then, frightened, she began racing around and around the pen with my brother astride of her, riding backwards, and trying desperately to keep his pail of swill from spilling.

About the third time around, the sow turned and dashed out of a hole that led into the hog yard. As she went out the small opening, Albert was scraped off, falling into the muck with the swill on top of him. Just at that critical moment, he looked up to see his wife taking in the whole show. Now why is it that wives always are around at the wrong time?

Dr. Earl E. Clarke, Dean of Students at Ithaca College, tells about some hogs owned by a neighbor for whom he sometimes worked when a boy on a North Dakota farm. This neighbor had the first silo for miles around. As all cattlemen now know, after corn is put into the silo, and if the bottom of the silo is not tight, a fermented juice will leak out for several days. It has been said, perhaps by someone speaking from experience, that this juice is so potent that a mouse who imbibes a little of it will chase a tomcat right up a tree.

"One day," said Earl, "when I was a boy and worked for this neighbor, I saw several of his half-grown pigs racing crazily all around the barnyard, jumping, squealing, and falling down, only to struggle to their feet again to run until they fell down again.

"Fascinated, I watched the pigs' crazy antics, wondering what in the world was the matter with them. Then, fearing that the pigs had all been struck by some awful disease, I ran to get the owner. He came on the run, watched the pigs for a few minutes, apparently puzzled and worried. Then he began to

236

laugh. 'They're drunk,' he yelled, 'just plain drunk. They've been drinking that silage juice. They'll be all right tomorrow but I'd hate to have their morning-after headache.' "

While I'm telling these hog stories, I might as well tell the one about the red-haired wag who, when he wanted to, would look like a fool. In the village where he lived, there were always some summer boarders who were only tolerated by the local folks because they brought some income into the neighborhood. On one occasion, our red-haired friend was trying to lead or drive a hog across the muddy road. Now, if you have had any experience with hogs, you will know that this is an almost impossible task. Just when our friend was having his hardest time leading, pushing, and swearing the hog across the road, a bunch of the summer boarders came along in a democrat wagon. To the vast amusement of the others, one of the boarders yelled, "One of your family?" The red-haired man straightened up, took off his ragged straw hat, put on his foolish look, and yelled back, "No. Just a summer boarder!"

On the home farm, and later when I farmed for myself, we seldom raised more than three or four hogs—all for pork and its by-products for home use. Home butchering was always an interesting but awesome event. We were always helped at butchering time by someone in the neighborhood who did the work regularly and was skilled at it.

The big iron kettle was hung over an outdoor fire, and it was the boys' job to carry and heat plenty of water. After the hog was killed, he was soused full length in the hogshead of hot water, which loosened his bristles. Then he was laid on a platform, and all hands joined in scraping the bristles off with sharp metal instruments in the shape of a candlestick.

The next operation was to hang the hog, head down, from a horizontal pole, open him, and remove and carefully save every part of the carcass. Even the intestines were saved and the leaf lard carefully removed from them and tried out on the kitchen stove. The hams and shoulders were cured in a solution of salt and saltpeter and later smoked in the little smokehouse over a smouldering fire of corn cobs. No modern, artificial curing and smoking of hams can produce the delicious flavor of a ham home-cured and smoked.

A large part of the hog was cut into convenient

sizes and went in the family pork barrels in a solution of salt and saltpeter to become the chief source of meat for the family throughout the entire year.

Some farm families were lucky enough to kill beef for family use, but we were glad to get steak or roast beef once a week from the local butcher's cart. I had so much salt pork when I was young that I have always been able since to give a good imitation of a hog squealing or grunting.

In recent years, the type of hog grown for market has been rapidly changing from the heavy, fat ones we used to grow to the leaner types. People, too, have changed, and a much leaner diet is in order for a population that does far less heavy labor than it did Day Before Yesterday.

The chief reason for a farm boy's interest in butchering time was the prospect of fresh meat every day, for a while at least, instead of salt pork.

But with the opening of the West, the hog business, like many other eastern farm enterprises, went west and became a great specialized commercial enterprise. The result has been that few hogs are now raised on the eastern farms, even for home use.

Not long ago, I visited a friend of mine in Wisconsin. Standing with him by a tight fence, I watched his drove of more than 100 hogs pastured on grass. Later in the season, the pigs would be finished off for market with a carefully balanced ration which would make them grow as much as possible in a short time without gaining too much fat.

As I looked at all those hogs, I marveled at the differences by which they are grown now as compared with the three or four we used to grow on eastern farms. We kept our hogs penned in a little house with just a small outside yard in which they were free to run. They had little or no access to pasture or other green feed. Pasturing was never practiced to any extent in the East. In early days, when it was available, our hogs were grown mostly on skim milk and then finished off chiefly with corn to make them as fat and heavy as possible. But now the business in the Midwest is a trade in itself. The special feeding techniques, including pasture and balanced rations, and the number of hogs on one of these farms would make my father and grandfather open their eyes in amazement.

## WHEN THE TORNADO STRUCK

An elderly lady who lived in New Hampshire wrote me once: "Weather is something we have a lot of, up here."

That same statement can be made for nearly every section of the United States, especially if you mean *violent* weather. I know of nothing more ominous in the North than the great black thunderclouds that come rolling up out of the western or northwestern sky near the end of a breathless day. Even the animals are uneasy, and when the storm is preceded by a violent wind, flashes of lightning, and the crashing of thunder, no wonder the farmer fears for his buildings and the timid crawl under their beds!

Hurricanes hit the North as well as the South. Don't I know! Along the Atlantic Coast and especially in New England, hurricanes have caused millions of dollars' worth of damage. I drove through some of the ruined country a day or so after the terrible storm of 1938, and I will never forget the havoc that I saw. It looked as if a gigantic roller had swept across the countryside, leveling about everything in its path. I saw beautiful apple orchards with every tree uprooted and whole forests in such tangled messes that it took years to clean them up.

Here in the northern part of the United States, we have blizzards that are exceedingly dangerous to be caught out in, but of all the violent demonstrations of old Mother Nature on the rampage, I think I would most fear those whirling funnel-shaped storms known as cyclones or tornadoes.

One of my daughters-in-law, Tenney Williams Eastman, who grew up in western Texas, tells me about a tornado that hit not far from her home there.

"Late in the afternoon, we knew that tornado clouds were building, but we didn't know of course whether it would hit the ground. Mother turned on the radio and soon learned that the people in the little village of Clyde were calling for all available doctors and ambulances. Dad immediately ran to a neighbor's home, for this neighbor had a sister living in Clyde. Dad and the neighbor drove to Clyde and found that the sister was safe. Then they spent hours trying to help the wounded and removing the dead from the terrible wreck. To add to the misery, it was raining hard as it always does with a tornado.

"The next morning, Mother and I went with Dad to do what we could to help. There was about a four-block area that was swept completely clean, including a one-block residential area and some fruit orchards. Not a single splinter, board or brick was left, nor was there any evidence of the human beings who had been there.

"About two hours after the tornado had passed, a search party found two little boys; a four-year-old and a six-month-old baby in a bar-ditch beside the highway, in water up to their necks. The four-year-old was holding the baby above the water and crying. These children had been in a car with their parents, trying to get to shelter before the storm struck. The little boys were about a quarter of a mile from where it was thought they were when the storm hit. No part of the car nor sign of the parents was ever found— no clothes, no bones, no nothing! Every single person above ground in this area was killed.

"At the edge of the storm, some houses were turned around on their foundations with maybe a room sliced off, or a roof lifted. A refrigerator was found in the top of a tree.

240

"Exactly 20 years to the day, another tornado struck the same area, but this time no one was killed. They had learned their lesson."

Lest I leave a wrong impression of Texas climate, let me add that Tenney says that out of the 365 days in the year, there will not be more than five or so when the sun doesn't shine at least a little. That would seem pretty good to a Northerner who sees so many dark days.

## FATHER AND THE GOLDEN GLOW

When I was a boy, ours was about the only lawn in the neghborhood that was kept mowed and green with old-time flowers bordering the yard and growing in the farm garden. Inside the house, we also had a bay window filled with house plants in the wintertime, supplemented by others blossoming in the kitchen windows. Looking back on it now, I realize that Mother certainly did have a "green thumb." Plants and flowers are like animals; they flourish with that little extra touch that comes with loving care. That goes for people, too.

Outdoors, Mother's flowers were the same as those her mother and great-grandmothers before her had grown: roses, of course, and sweet peas, pansies, phlox, zinnias, nasturtiums, petunias, and marigolds. We did not have delphiniums, but they are one of the oldest and most beautiful of the perennials. It is reported that when one of the Pharaoh's tombs was opened in recent years, a delphinium stalk was found with blossoms still showing some of their lovely color after 2,000 years. That was quite a spell ago, so I can't exactly remember placing those flowers with Pharaoh's body when he was entombed—but then, my memory is not as good as it used to be!

Among the outdoor flowers of which Mother was particularly fond was a bunch of golden glow. This flower grows in a clump on slender stalks, sometimes six feet high. It has a beautiful yellow or golden blossom that lasts a long time in late summer and fall.

In the summertime, it was Father's habit to get up very early in the morning before the rest of us, to go after the cows. After his death, it always saddened me to remember that we lazy boys let Father get the cows in the morning and too often let him climb the steep hill pasture to bring them home at night. In his later years, Father used a long stick for a cane when he climbed that hill, very slowly, and I realized

—when it was too late—that he had to go slowly because he had heart trouble.

One early morning when Father was bringing home the cows, I listened from my open bedroom window, as he talked to them to keep them in order. He was speaking in a quiet tone of voice so as not to disturb Mother, who had not been feeling too well. The herd rumbled across the bridge over the creek and then, suddenly, I heard Father yell at the cows in an excited tone of voice. Jumping out of bed, I ran to a window to see what was the matter. The cows had gotten out of control and instead of following their usual path to the barn, they had broken across Mother's nice lawn and run right through the clump of golden glow, completely ruining it. By the time I pulled on my overalls and shirt, Father had rounded up the cows and put them into the stable. We did the milking and other chores that morning in silence, and went reluctantly to the house for breakfast.

For years, Mother had asked Father to put a wire around the front yard, but he had never gotten around to doing it. So, naturally, we wondered what Mother would have to say about her precious golden glow. One of the interesting, if not always pleasant, characteristics about women is that you never can be sure just what their reactions will be to life's crises, large or small. A heavy silence hung over the breakfast table that morning, but near the end of the meal, Mother arose, went around to stand by Father's side, and put her arm around his shoulders.

"Forget it, Charlie," she said kindly. "The golden glow was about done for this year anyway and it will grow again next year."

## SLEEPING WITH ALBERT

If you were a boy, did you ever have to sleep with a brother on a hot summer night on a lumpy straw mattress that rolled you both toward the middle? I came home on one such night from working for a neighbor after a long, hot day in the hayfield. The upstairs bedrooms in the farmhouse were always hot in the summertime. My younger brother had a habit of whispering to himself, just before he went to sleep, about everything that had happened to him during the day, and that whispering drove me frantic.

On that particular night, I was tired and hot. The whispering, when I was trying to get to sleep, was just the last straw. So, after remonstrating with Albert in language that should have moved mountains—all to no avail—I kicked him out of the bed. But he promptly got back in and kicked me out. Then we engaged in a free-for-all. We did not try to hit each other; I was a little bigger and dragged him out of the room. But, like the cat in the old song, he always came back.

After this process had been repeated several times, the noise aroused the rest of the family and they came upstairs on the run and separated us. I went to the barn and slept in the haymow for the rest of the night, but that hot hay in the top of the barn was no improvement over the lumpy old bed.

Albert—my younger brother, who was as good a man as I have ever known—died not long ago, and I only wish that I could sleep with him now, whispering and all.

# CHAPTER TWENTY-SEVEN

# UNTIL DEATH DO US PART

Young people used to get fun from hornings and shivarees when a couple in the village or country got married. Money was usually scarce, so many young married couples were financially unable to take long honeymoon trips. Instead, they spent their honeymoon at their parents' home or immediately went to housekeeping in their new home. This gave the young men of the neighborhood the opportunity to gather on the first night where the couple was staying, and with horns, cymbals, old pans and other noise-making gadgets, raise an unholy racket that lasted far into the night and that could be heard in the next world.

At one such horning, described by one of my grandmothers, the noise continued until she and the newly married couple went to the door and invited the whole crowd in for refreshments, which had been previously prepared in anticipation of just such an event.

* * *

What was an old-time courtship and marriage like?

In September 1902, I entered a teachers' training class to study for a certificate to teach in the public schools of the state. During the first morning session, I found a note on my desk which read, "Didn't your uncle marry my aunt?" The note was signed, Belle Rockefeller. I had never seen the girl before, but of course I knew about her. And after getting that note, I paid more attention to looking at her than I did to the teacher or the other members of the class. I was justified, and I've been looking ever since. She was beautiful—and of course I was intrigued because, in a manner of speaking, she was a member of the family. *That* was the beginning of a courtship that lasted four years, and of a marriage that has lasted 57 years, surviving all the ups and downs of more

changes and complications in the life around us then in any other similar period in human history.

That waiting period of four years was tough. When young college students whom I am counseling tell me how lonesome they are for a girl or boy friend back home, I can be very sympathetic, remembering how difficult it was for Belle and me to see each other in the horse-and-buggy days when we were 20 miles apart most of the time.

During the first part of our acquaintance—before Belle would consent to an engagement—it was rough going for me, so much so, that I wonder now how I ever got my work done. Belle lived in a distant village and commuted the 20 miles back and forth every day to the school we attended. At the end of the school day, I had to work, so the village boys (darn them!) could carry Belle's books to the station and sit with her until train time. Added to my misery was the fact that some of the boys also commuted and could ride with her on the train every day.

One day after school, I skipped work in order to be near Belle in the schoolroom before train time and perhaps walk her to the station, even if there were other boys present. While there, I leaned on the edge of a big table covered with bottles filled with chemicals—and table, boy, and expensive chemicals all crashed to the floor in a bad mess. I'm sure that I didn't make a very good impression on Belle, but *that* was not the worst of it. One of the hardest things I have ever had to do was see the principal, Mr. J.S. Kingsley, and tell him what had happened. God bless the memory of that man for his understanding heart! He didn't scold; he didn't criticize.

If you were a farm boy, you probably have rested for a few minutes from your work in the fields and lain in the shade of a tree where the sun made dappled shadows on the ground around you. If so, no doubt you have also done as I did—held your holey old straw hat over your face and wondered and dreamed about your girl and what life is all about. I remember one particular lonesome summer when I frequently did just that, after perhaps reading the letter in my pocket until it was worn from handling, and then watch the sunbeams through my hat, while I longed—only as a boy can long—to see the girl I loved.

The lonesome times were more than overbalanced by the wholesome fun we had when we could get together. One time, I hired a tandem bicycle, now a curiosity. Putting Belle on the back seat, we started for my home, going the long way around the mountain instead of over. I guess I never worked harder in my life than I did trying to pump that more-or-less worn-out wheel. Finally, a little irritated, I told her that she wasn't doing her part but was letting me do all the pumping. But just as vigorously, she claimed that I was the one who was loafing. So we both got off, rested awhile, and *walked* all the rest of the way, pushing the darn thing by hand. In spite of that somewhat awkward experience, I think we have done a pretty good job of "riding in tandem" ever since.

There was another time in our engagement when we started over the hills from Belle's home, with our own separate bicycles, to visit my uncle and her aunt (our mutual relatives). As we were going down a long hill, I suddenly saw and heard Belle go by me on her wheel, just as if I were standing still. Her bicycle had run away with her. She landed at the foot of the hill in a patch of blackberry bushes. Much concerned and scared, I got to her as fast as I could, but soon found out that nothing except her dignity and temper had been injured. I kept very still for the rest of the trip, since some way or other, woman-like, she thought that I was to blame. But by the time we arrived at Uncle's house, the clouds had cleared.

Time passed and we both became teachers in widely separated schools, so the lonesomeness and longing grew until finally, after four long years (and believe me, years can be long for the young), when I was 21, we were married.

It was a Sunday in early spring. We had spent a glorious weekend at my parents' home. Late, on that day of April 8, 1906, we started out to walk the five miles over the mountain to the village where we first met. From there we would go to schools where we would teach the next morning. On top of the hill —and I know the *exact* spot—I said to Belle, "Let's get married." And by golly, after years of telling me that we were not old enough, she agreed! Right then and there, we planned to get married on that very same day. Arriving in the village, we went to the home of our pastor, a long-time friend of mine, and asked him to marry us.

"Right here and now?" he asked, surprised. And we answered, "Yes!" After a moment's thought, he said, "I have a better plan."

246

Noting the look of disappointment on my face, he hastened to explain. "We're having a union meeting of the congregations in this part of the county in my church tonight. I have been preparing for it for a long time. The church will be filled to capacity, and you will have a big church wedding all prepared for you. All you need to do is sit in the front pew and at the close of the services, I will call you before me and marry you."

After some hesitation, we agreed. To this day, I can't remember a single word of that pastor's sermon. Very likely it was a wonderful one for, as he said, he had been preparing it for a long time. I sat with Belle in a front pew more scared than I have ever been before or since. I don't recall what he said in the wedding ceremony either, but it must have been all right, for we have a certificate that says so.

If the pastor wanted to surprise his congregation, he certainly succeeded. A friend of mine, an older man, told me afterwards that right in the middle of the ceremony, he had started to jump to his feet, thinking that the minister had made the mistake of using the wedding ceremony when he really meant just to take us into the church membership. But it was no mistake, thank God, for it worked, in spite of the hard going sometimes that comes to all of us.

The next morning, we got up early and I took the train to school where I was teaching, and Belle took the stagecoach to her school. When we finally did get together the next September as teachers in the same school, we set up housekeeping in a three-room apartment with a few pieces of second-hand furniture from both of our parents' homes.

One time when we were first married, I invited a school supervisor from the State Education Department to supper. I wanted very much to make a good impression on him. During the course of the meal, I asked Belle several times to get more spoons. After repeated kickings under the table—kickings which registered on my shins but not on my brain—Belle said, "If you must know, *there are no more spoons!*" Then we all laughed. God help people who can't laugh off their trivial and unimportant annoyances. There is enough to be serious about.

So Belle and I have laughed together and cried together since that long-ago day when I first saw her, and when she put the little note on my desk. We lost two children, but Donald, George, and Robert are still with us, and we with them, with their wives who are our beloved daughters, with our seven grandchildren and two great-grandchildren— "all for one and one for all."

Yesterday, I met my friend, Mr. Fred Rumsey, and we stopped to visit. As of this writing, Fred is 92 years old and his wife is just a little younger. He was bursting with enthusiasm and told me that he was doing just as much business per month as he ever had.

\* \* \*

How wonderful it would be if marriages like the Rumseys' were not so rare. Of all the problems which beset us modern Americans, there is none more tragic or more dangerous to our whole social structure than the fact that so many marriages fail. Even if they don't end in divorce or separation, as bad or worse are the thousands of men and women still living together with constant misunderstanding and quarreling that often approaches actual hate.

Love we have—or think we have—when we become engaged. It makes the engagement and honeymoon glorious, but then, sad to relate, in too many cases, instead of deepening and purifying our love, we

247

The long road was sometimes rough and steep for Belle and me, but we walked it together.

fail with the coming years to keep it bright and shining; we fail to "live happily ever after" and marriage indeed becomes a sentence and not a glorification.

What happens? Why do so many marriages fail?

I am convinced that, with many marriages, the biggest source of trouble is the lack of communication and the failure to share all experiences. During the engagement period and the early years of marriage, you talk about and share everything. You make it a point to remember all the things that may be of interest to the other and you can hardly wait to tell your partner about them. As your marriage progresses, there should be more and more mutual interests to share. But do we share them?

When the country was young, and most of the young people were farmers, the whole family had a part in the farm business. Problems were talked over at mealtime and during the long evenings. There was much more family togetherness than there is now. Today, millions of married women work outside the home at one job, while their husbands work at another. It is not always good, of course, to bring outside work troubles or problems into the home, but there are many things of great interest in connection with almost any job that could be talked over with interest at home.

In my own home, as we sit around the breakfast table in the morning and at dinner, we have for many years visited on any one of a hundred subjects, thus sharing interests and points of view.

It is not to be expected that all the marriage days will be as bright as those of the honeymoon. There will of course be troubles, worries, and responsibilities, all of which can be lightened when shared by a partner. All of us being human, there is sure to be some bickering and misunderstandings, no matter how hard we try. The man who said that he had lived 40 years with his wife Maria with never a cross word is a darn liar! But the big point to remember, when there is some minor or major misunderstanding, is that there is nothing as important as keeping your love alive, and nothing much worse than going to sleep at night with bitterness and resentment in your heart. One friend told me that his most important recipe for marriage happiness was—no matter what had happened during the day, what misunderstanding there had been—he and his wife made sure to kiss each other goodnight before they went to sleep.

The love that exists during the honeymoon can be deepened and made to last if one is wise enough to realize that happiness, like all other things of great worth, must be constantly worked for. This means, among other things, *talking things over*—communicating not only on matters outside the home but including the most intimate relations between partners, as well as our work, our finances, and our children. Never, never should we let our marriage get so matter-of-fact that we neglect to tell and show every day how much we love our partner.

Looking back at Day Before Yesterday gives us about the only perspective, the only glimpse of what Tomorrow may be like. There have been more changes during the lifetime of my generation than have ever occurred in the history of mankind. With that perspective, I close this visit with you on an optimistic note. I predict that changes for the good, material and spiritual, have only just started. So far, we have just scratched the surface. Your children, grandchildren, and mine will live to see a Day After Tomorrow as different from today as today is from Day Before Yesterday.

# PICTURE CREDITS

Photo on page 3, Courtesy, New York State Historical Association, Cooperstown, N.Y.

Photo on page 5, Courtesy, New York State Historical Association, Cooperstown, N.Y.

Photo on page 7, Courtesy, J. W. McManigal, Horton, Kansas

Photo on pages 12 and 13, Courtesy, New York State Historical Association, Cooperstown, N.Y.

Photo on page 23, Courtesy, U.S.D.A. Photograph

Photo on page 30, Courtesy, Grace Munch, Brooktondale, N.Y.

Photo on page 45, Courtesy, Ruth B. Runyon, Sherburne, N.Y.

Photo on page 58, Courtesy, *American Agriculturist*

Photo on page 64, Courtesy, E. E. Bliss, Taunton, Mass.

Photo on page 65, Courtesy, Albert W. Dietz, N. Pitcher, N.Y.

Photo on page 66, Courtesy, *American Agriculturist*

Photo on page 71, Courtesy, DeWitt Historical Society, Ithaca, N.Y.

Photo on page 74, Courtesy, DeWitt Historical Society, Ithaca, N.Y.

Photo on page 82, Courtesy, J. W. McManigal, Horton, Kansas

Photo on page 93, Courtesy, U.S.D.A. Photograph

Photo on page 98, Courtesy, DeWitt Historical Society, Ithaca, N.Y.

Photo on page 100, Courtesy, DeWitt Historical Society, Ithaca, N.Y.

Photo on page 114, Courtesy, New York State College of Agriculture

Photo on page 139, Courtesy, Charles Vorhis

Photo on page 143, Courtesy, New York State Historical Association, Cooperstown, N.Y.

Photo on page 157, Courtesy, New York State Historical Association, Cooperstown, N.Y.

Photo on page 160, Courtesy, New York State Historical Association, Cooperstown, N.Y.

Photo on page 167, Courtesy, Albert W. Dietz, N. Pitcher, N.Y.

Photo on page 170, Courtesy, Mrs. Caroline Underhill, Batavia, N.Y.

Photo on page 171, Courtesy, Lawrence H. Champeau

Photo on page 176, Courtesy, N.Y. State Historical Association, Cooperstown, N.Y.

Photo on page 183, Courtesy, New England Homestead

Photo on page 188, Courtesy, Farmers' Museum, Cooperstown, N.Y.

Photo on page 190, Courtesy, Alfred Munch, Brooktondale, N.Y.

Photo on page 205, Courtesy, New York State College of Agriculture

Photo on page 207, Courtesy, New York State College of Agriculture

Photo on page 210 left, Courtesy, J. I. Case Co.

Photo on page 210 right, Courtesy, International Harvester Co.

Photo on page 211 left, Courtesy, New York State Historical Association, Cooperstown, N.Y.

Photo on page 211 right, Courtesy, F. T. Davis, Le Raysville, Pa.

Photo on page 221, Courtesy, United States Department of Agriculture